2B

FOUR CORNERS

Second Edition

Student's Book
with Digital Pack

JACK C. RICHARDS & DAVID BOHLKE

Shaftesbury Road, Cambridge CB2 8EA, United Kingdom

One Liberty Plaza, 20th Floor, New York, NY 10006, USA

477 Williamstown Road, Port Melbourne, VIC 3207, Australia

314–321, 3rd Floor, Plot 3, Splendor Forum, Jasola District Centre, New Delhi – 110025, India

103 Penang Road, #05–06/07, Visioncrest Commercial, Singapore 238467

Cambridge University Press & Assessment is a department of the University of Cambridge.

We share the University's mission to contribute to society through the pursuit of education, learning and research at the highest international levels of excellence.

www.cambridge.org
Information on this title: www.cambridge.org/9781009286466

First published 2012
Second edition 2019

20 19 18 17 16 15 14 13 12 11 10 9 8 7 6 5 4 3 2 1

Printed in Malaysia by Vivar Printing

A catalogue record for this publication is available from the British Library

ISBN 978-1-009-28633-6 Student's Book with Digital Pack 2
ISBN 978-1-009-28645-9 Student's Book with Digital Pack 2A
ISBN 978-1-009-28646-6 Student's Book with Digital Pack 2B
ISBN 978-1-108-65228-5 Teacher's Edition with Complete Assessment Program 2
ISBN 978-1-009-28647-3 Full Contact with Digital Pack 2
ISBN 978-1-009-28648-0 Full Contact with Digital Pack 2A
ISBN 978-1-009-28649-7 Full Contact with Digital Pack 2B
ISBN 978-1-009-28594-0 Presentation Plus Level 2

Additional resources for this publication at www.cambridge.org/fourcorners

Authors' acknowledgments

Many people contributed to the development of *Four Corners*. The authors and publisher would like to particularly thank the following **reviewers**:

Nele Noe, **Academy for Educational Development, Qatar Independent Secondary School for Girls**, Doha, Qatar; Pablo Stucchi, **Antonio Raimondi School** and **Instituto San Ignacio de Loyola**, Lima, Peru; **Nadeen Katz, Asia University, Tokyo, Japan;** Tim Vandenhoek, **Asia University**, Tokyo, Japan; Celso Frade and Sonia Maria Baccari de Godoy, **Associação Alumni**, São Paulo, Brazil; Rosane Bandeira, **Atlanta Idiomas**, Manaus, Brazil; Cacilda Reis da Silva, **Atlanta Idiomas**, Manaus, Brazil; Gretta Sicsu, **Atlanta Idiomas**, Manaus, Brazil; Naila Maria Cañiso Ferreira, **Atlanta Idiomas**, Manaus, Brazil; Hothnã Moraes de Souza Neto, **Atlanta Idiomas**, Manaus, Brazil; Jacqueline Kurtzious, **Atlanta Idiomas**, Manaus, Brazil; José Menezes Ribeiro Neto, **Atlanta Idiomas**, Manaus, Brazil; Sheila Ribeiro Cordeiro, **Atlanta Idiomas**, Manaus, Brazil; Juliana Fernandes, **Atlanta Idiomas**, Manaus, Brazil; Aline Alexandrina da Silva, **Atlanta Idiomas**, Manaus, Brazil; Kari Miller, **Binational Center**, Quito, Ecuador; Alex K. Oliveira, **Boston University**, Boston, MA, USA; Noriko Furuya, **Bunka Gakuen University**, Tokyo, Japan; Robert Hickling, **Bunka Gakuen University**, Tokyo, Japan; John D. Owen, **Bunka Gakuen University**, Tokyo, Japan; Elisabeth Blom, **Casa Thomas Jefferson**, Brasília, Brazil; Lucilena Oliveira Andrade, **Centro Cultural Brasil Estados Unidos (CCBEU Belém)**, Belém, Brazil; Marcelo Franco Borges, **Centro Cultural Brasil Estados Unidos (CCBEU Belém)**, Belém, Brazil; Geysa de Azevedo Moreira, **Centro Cultural Brasil Estados Unidos (CCBEU Belém)**, Belém, Brazil; Anderson Felipe Barbosa Negrão, **Centro Cultural Brasil Estados Unidos (CCBEU Belém)**, Belém, Brazil; Henry Grant, **CCBEU – Campinas**, Campinas, Brazil; Maria do Rosário, **CCBEU – Franca**, Franca, Brazil; Ane Cibele Palma, **CCBEU Inter Americano**, Curitiba, Brazil; Elen Flavia Penques da Costa, **Centro de Cultura Idiomas – Taubaté**, Taubaté, Brazil; Inara Lúcia Castillo Couto, **CEL LEP – São Paulo**, São Paulo, Brazil; Sonia Patricia Cardoso, **Centro de Idiomas Universidad Manuela Beltrán**, Barrio Cedritos, Colombia; Geraldine Itiago Losada, **Centro Universitario Grupo Sol (Musali)**, Mexico City, Mexico; Nick Hilmers, **DePaul University**, Chicago, IL, USA; Monica L. Montemayor Menchaca, **EDIMSA**, Metepec, Mexico; Angela Whitby, **Edu-Idiomas Language School**, Cholula, Puebla, Mexico; Mary Segovia, **El Monte Rosemead Adult School**, Rosemead, CA, USA; Dr. Deborah Aldred, **ELS Language Centers, Middle East Region**, Abu Dhabi, United Arab Emirates; Leslie Lott, **Embassy CES**, Ft. Lauderdale, FL, USA; M. Martha Lengeling, **Escuela de Idiomas**, Guanajuato, Mexico; Pablo Frias, **Escuela de Idiomas UNAPEC**, Santo Domingo, Dominican Republic; Tracy Vanderhoek, **ESL Language Center**, Toronto, Canada; Kris Vicca and Michael McCollister, **Feng Chia University**, Taichung, Taiwan; Flávia Patricia do Nascimento Martins, **First Idiomas**, Sorocaba, Brazil; Andrea Taylor, **Florida State University in Panama**, Panamá, Panama; Carlos Lizárraga González, **Groupo Educativo Angloamericano**, Mexico City, Mexico; Bo-Kyung Lee, **Hankuk University of Foreign Studies**, Seoul, South Korea; Dr. Martin Endley, **Hanyang University**, Seoul, South Korea; Mauro Luiz Pinheiro, **IBEU Ceará**, Ceará, Brazil; Ana Lúcia da Costa Maia de Almeida, **IBEU Copacabana**, Copacabana, Brazil; Maristela Silva, **ICBEU Manaus**, Manaus, Brazil; Magaly Mendes Lemos, **ICBEU São José dos Campos**, São José dos Campos, Brazil; Augusto Pelligrini Filho, **ICBEU São Luis**, São Luis, Brazil; Leonardo Mercado, **ICPNA**, Lima, Peru; Lucia Rangel Lugo, **Instituto Tecnológico de San Luis Potosí**, San Luis Potosí, Mexico; Maria Guadalupe Hernández Lozada, **Instituto Tecnológico de Tlalnepantla**, Tlalnepantla de Baz, Mexico; Karen Stewart, **International House Veracruz**, Veracruz, Mexico; Tom David, **Japan College of Foreign Languages**, Tokyo, Japan; Andy Burki, **Korea University, International Foreign Language School**, Seoul, South Korea; Jinseo Noh, **Kwangwoon University**, Seoul, South Korea; Neil Donachey, **La Salle Junior and Senior High School**, Kagoshima, Japan; Rich Hollingworth, **La Salle Junior and Senior High School**, Kagoshima, Japan; Quentin Kum, **La Salle Junior and Senior High School**, Kagoshima, Japan; Geoff Oliver, **La Salle Junior and Senior High School**, Kagoshima, Japan; Martin Williams, **La Salle Junior and Senior High School**, Kagoshima, Japan; Nadezhda Nazarenko, **Lone Star College**, Houston, TX, USA; Carolyn Ho, **Lone Star College-Cy-Fair**, Cypress, TX, USA; Kaoru Kuwajima, Meijo University, Nagoya, Japan; Alice Ya-fen Chou, **National Taiwan University of Science and Technology**, Taipei, Taiwan; Raymond Dreyer, **Northern Essex Community College**, Lawrence, MA, USA; Mary Keter Terzian Megale, **One Way Línguas-Suzano**, São Paulo, Brazil; B. Greg Dunne, **Osaka Shoin Women's University**, Higashi-Osaka, Japan; Robert Maran, **Osaka Shoin Women's University**, Higashi-Osaka, Japan; Bonnie Cheeseman, **Pasadena Community College** and **UCLA American Language Center**, Los Angeles, CA, USA; Simon Banha, **Phil Young's English School**, Curitiba, Brazil; Oh Jun Il, **Pukyong National University**, Busan, South Korea; Carmen Gehrke, **Quatrum English Schools**, Porto Alegre, Brazil; John Duplice, **Rikkyo University**, Tokyo, Japan; Wilzania da Silva Nascimento, **Senac**, Manaus, Brazil; Miva Silva Kingston, **Senac**, Manaus, Brazil; Lais Lima, **Senac**, Manaus, Brazil; Yuan-hsun Chuang, **Soo Chow University**, Taipei, Taiwan; Mengjiao Wu, Shanghai Maritime University, Shanghai, China; Wen hsiang Su, **Shih Chien University Kaohsiung Campus**, Kaohsiung, Taiwan; Lynne Kim, **Sun Moon University (Institute for Language Education)**, Cheon An City, Chung Nam, South Korea; Regina Ramalho, **Talken English School**, Curitiba, Brazil; Tatiana Mendonça, **Talken English School**, Curitiba, Brazil; Ricardo Todeschini, **Talken English School**, Curitiba, Brazil; Monica Carvalho da Rocha, **Talken English School**, Joinville, Brazil; Karina Schoene, **Talken English School**, Joinville, Brazil; Diaña Peña Munoz and Zira Kuri, **The Anglo**, Mexico City, Mexico; Christopher Modell, **Tokai University**, Tokyo, Japan; Song-won Kim, **TTI (Teacher's Training Institute)**, Seoul, South Korea; Nancy Alarcón, **UNAM FES Zaragoza Language Center**, Mexico City, Mexico; Laura Emilia Fierro López, **Universidad Autónoma de Baja California**, Mexicali, Mexico; María del Rocío Domínguez Gaona, **Universidad Autónoma de Baja California**, Tijuana, Mexico; Saul Santos Garcia, **Universidad Autónoma de Nayarit**, Nayarit, Mexico; Christian Meléndez, **Universidad Católica de El Salvador**, San Salvador, El Salvador; Irasema Mora Pablo, **Universidad de Guanajuato**, Guanajuato, Mexico; Alberto Peto, **Universidad de Oaxaca**, Tehuantepec, Mexico; Carolina Rodriguez Beltan, **Universidad Manuela Beltrán, Centro Colombo Americano**, and **Universidad Jorge Tadeo Lozano**, Bogotá, Colombia; Nidia Milena Molina Rodriguez, **Universidad Manuela Beltrán** and **Universidad Militar Nueva Granada**, Bogotá, Colombia; Yolima Perez Arias, **Universidad Nacional de Colombia**, Bogotá, Colombia; Héctor Vázquez García, **Universidad Nacional Autónoma de Mexico**, Mexico City, Mexico; Pilar Barrera, **Universidad Técnica de Ambato**, Ambato, Ecuador; Doborah Hulston, **University of Regina**, Regina, Canada; Rebecca J. Shelton, **Valparaiso University, Interlink Language Center**, Valparaiso, IN, USA; Tae Lee, **Yonsei University**, Seodaemun-gu, Seoul, South Korea; Claudia Thereza Nascimento Mendes, **York Language Institute**, Rio de Janeiro, Brazil; Jamila Jenny Hakam, **ELT Consultant**, Muscat, Oman; Stephanie Smith, **ELT Consultant**, Austin, TX, USA.

Scope and sequence

LEVEL 2	Learning outcomes	Grammar	Vocabulary
Unit 7 Pages 65–74			
Shopping A *It's lighter and thinner.* B *Would you take $10?* C *This hat is too small.* D *A shopper's paradise*	**Students can...** ☑ describe and compare products ☑ bargain ☑ describe how clothing looks and fits ☑ discuss good places to shop	Comparative adjectives *Enough* and *too*	Opposites Adjectives to describe clothing
Unit 8 Pages 75–84			
Fun in the city A *You shouldn't miss it!* B *I'd recommend going . . .* C *The best and the worst* D *The best place to go*	**Students can...** ☑ say what people should do in a city ☑ ask for and give a recommendation ☑ make comparisons about their city ☑ discuss aspects of a city	*Should* for recommendations; *can* for possibility Superlative adjectives	Places to see Adjectives to describe
Unit 9 Pages 85–94			
People A *Where was he born?* B *I'm not sure, but I think . . .* C *People I admire* D *Making a difference*	**Students can...** ☑ ask and talk about people from the past ☑ express certainty and uncertainty ☑ describe people they admire ☑ describe people who made a difference	*Was / were* born; past of *be* Simple past; *ago*	Careers Personality adjectives
Unit 10 Pages 95–104			
In a restaurant A *The ice cream is fantastic!* B *I'll have the fish, please.* C *Have you ever . . .?* D *Restaurant experiences*	**Students can...** ☑ talk about menus and eating out ☑ order food in a restaurant ☑ ask about and describe food experiences ☑ describe restaurant experiences	Articles Present perfect for experience	Menu items Interesting food
Unit 11 Pages 105–114			
Entertainment A *I'm not a fan of dramas.* B *Any suggestions?* C *All of us love music.* D *Singing shows around the world*	**Students can...** ☑ talk about their movie habits and opinions ☑ ask for and give suggestions ☑ report the results of a survey ☑ describe important singers and musicians	*So, too, either,* and *neither* Determiners	Types of movies Types of music
Unit 12 Pages 115–124			
Time for a change A *Personal change* B *I'm happy to hear that!* C *I think I'll get a job.* D *Dreams and aspirations*	**Students can...** ☑ give reasons for personal changes ☑ react to good and bad news ☑ make predictions about the future ☑ discuss their dreams for the future	Infinitives of purpose *Will* for predictions; *may, might* for possibility	Personal goals Milestones

Functional language	Listening and Pronunciation	Reading and Writing	Speaking
Interactions: Bargaining for a lower price Suggesting a different price	**Listening:** Bargaining at a yard sale A weekend market in London **Pronunciation:** Linked sounds	**Reading:** "Chatucak Weekend Market" A webpage **Writing:** An interesting market	• Comparison of two products • *Keep talking*: Comparing several products • Role play of a bargaining situation • Discussion about clothes • *Keep talking*: Different clothing items • Discussion about good places to shop
Interactions: Asking for a recommendation Giving a recommendation	**Listening:** Cities At a tourist information desk **Pronunciation:** Word stress	**Reading:** "Austin or San Antonio?" A message board **Writing:** A message board	• Discussion about things to do in one day • *Keep talking*: Discussion of possible things to do • Role play at a tourist information desk • Comparison of places in a town or a city • *Keep talking*: City quiz • Discussion about aspects of a city
Interactions: Expressing certainty Expressing uncertainty	**Listening:** Friends playing a board game People who made a difference **Pronunciation:** Simple past *-ed* endings	**Reading:** "A Different Kind of Banker" A biography **Writing:** A biography	• Guessing game about famous people • *Keep talking*: Information gap activity about people from the past • Group quiz about famous people • Descriptions of admirable people • *Keep talking*: Discussion about inspiring people • Description of a person who made a difference
Interactions: Ordering food Checking information	**Listening:** Customers ordering food Restaurant impressions **Pronunciation:** *The* before vowel and consonant sounds	**Reading:** "Restaurants with a Difference" A webpage **Writing:** A review	• Discussion about eating out • *Keep talking*: A menu • Role play of a restaurant situation • Discussion about food experiences • *Keep talking*: Board game about food experiences • Restaurant recommendations
Interactions: Asking for suggestions Giving a suggestion	**Listening:** Fun things to do An influential world musician **Pronunciation:** Reduction of *of*	**Reading:** "Everybody Loves a Sing-Off" An online article **Writing:** A popular musician	• Movie talk • *Keep talking*: Movie favorites • Suggestions about the weekend • Class musical preferences • *Keep talking*: Class survey about music • A playlist
Interactions: Reacting to bad news Reacting to good news	**Listening:** Sharing news An interview with an athlete **Pronunciation:** Contraction of *will*	**Reading:** "An Olympic Dream Flies High" An online article **Writing:** A dream come true	• Discussion about changes • *Keep talking*: Reasons for doing things • Good news and bad news • Predictions about the future • *Keep talking*: Predictions about next year • Dream planner

Welcome

1 Working with a partner

A 🎧 Complete the conversations with the correct sentences. Then listen and check your answers.

- Can I borrow your pen?
- Let's compare our answers!
- Whose turn is it?
- Are you ready?

B PAIR WORK Practice the conversations.

2 Asking for help

A Match the questions and answers. Then practice with a partner.

1	How do you spell this word?	_d_	a	You say "welcome."
2	How do you pronounce this word?	_____	b	It means "not common."
3	What does this word mean?	_____	c	/ˈhɑbi/ (hobby).
4	How do you say *bienvenidos* in English?	_____	d	I-N-T-E-R-A-C-T-I-O-N-S.

B Write these four questions in the conversations. Then compare with a partner.

> What does this word mean?   How do you say *Boa sorte* in English?
> How do you pronounce this word?   How do you spell your first name?

1 A _____

   B /ˈkɑntɛkst/ (context).

   A Oh, that's easy!

2 A _____

   B I think it means "working together."

   A Just like us!

3 A _____

   B E-M-I-K-O.

   A That's a nice name.

4 A _____

   B You say "Good luck."

   A I see. Well, good luck!

C 🎧 Listen and check your answers. Then practice the conversations with a partner.

3 Speaking Do you know?

A `PAIR WORK` Think of two English words you know. Ask your partner about them.

A: What *does* the word *kitten* mean?

B: It means "baby cat."

B `PAIR WORK` Look at a page in the book and find two words. Write one word in each blank. Ask about the words.

How do you spell this word?   How do you pronounce this word?

_____   _____

C `GROUP WORK` Think of words or expressions that you want to know in English. Ask your group how to say them. Can they answer?

A: How *do* you say _____ in English?

B: You say "_____ ."

> I can ask questions about English words. ✓

Classroom language

A Write these actions below the correct picture. Then compare with a partner.

Close your books.	Look at the picture.	Turn to page . . .
Listen.	✓ Open your books.	Work in groups.
Look at the board.	Raise your hand.	Work in pairs.

1 _____Open your books._____

2 _____

3 _____

4 _____

5 _____

6 _____

7 _____

8 _____

9 _____

A: What's number one?

B: It's . . .

B 🎧 Listen and check your answers.

C 🎧 Listen to seven of the actions. Do each one.

4

7 Shopping

Warm up

A Describe the pictures. How many things can you name?

B Where do you usually shop? What do you like to buy?

A It's lighter and thinner.

1 Vocabulary Opposites

A 🎧 Label the pictures with the correct words. Then listen and check your answers.

| big expensive heavy loud slow thick |

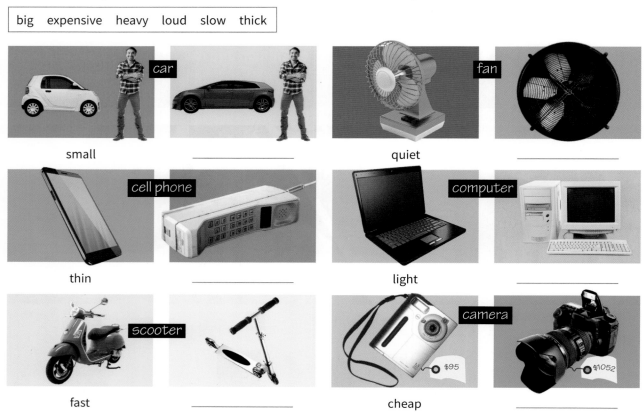

small _____   quiet _____

thin _____   light _____

fast _____   cheap _____

B **PAIR WORK** Use the words in Part A to describe things you own. Tell your partner.

"My cell phone is thin and light."

2 Language in context Which is better?

A 🎧 Read the message board. Then label the pictures.

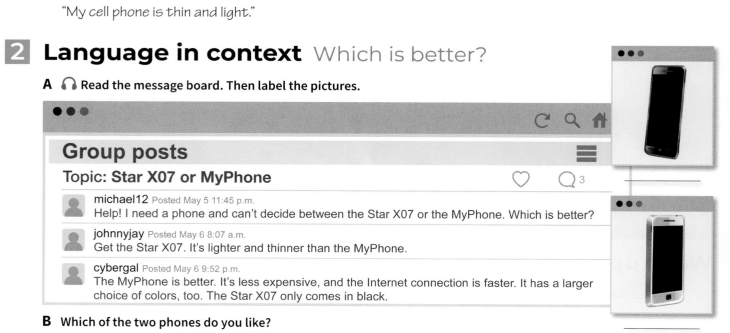

Group posts

Topic: **Star X07 or MyPhone**   ♡   ⬚ 3

michael12 Posted May 5 11:45 p.m.
Help! I need a phone and can't decide between the Star X07 or the MyPhone. Which is better?

johnnyjay Posted May 6 8:07 a.m.
Get the Star X07. It's lighter and thinner than the MyPhone.

cybergal Posted May 6 9:52 p.m.
The MyPhone is better. It's less expensive, and the Internet connection is faster. It has a larger choice of colors, too. The Star X07 only comes in black.

B Which of the two phones do you like?

3 Grammar 🎧 Comparative adjectives

The Star X07 is **lighter than** the MyPhone.

The MyPhone is **heavier than** the Star X07.

Which cell phone is **more expensive**?

 The Star X07 is **more expensive than** the MyPhone.

 The MyPhone is **less expensive than** the Star X07.

Is the MyPhone **better than** the Star X07?

No, I don't think it's **better**. It's **worse**.

Adjective	Comparative
light	light**er**
nice	nic**er**
thin	thin**ner**
heavy	heav**ier**
difficult	**more / less** difficult
good	**better**
bad	**worse**

Complete the sentences with the correct comparative form. Add *than* if necessary. Then compare with a partner.

1 Is your new printer _____ (fast) your old one?

2 Are desktop computers always _____ (heavy) laptops?

3 This new camera is really cheap! It's _____ (expensive) than my old one.

4 I like this TV, but I think I want a _____ (big) one.

5 This phone has a big screen, so it's _____ (expensive) than other phones.

6 My new camera isn't _____ (good) my old one. In fact,
   it's _____ (bad)!

4 Speaking Let's compare

A PAIR WORK **Compare these products. How many sentences can you make?**

Car A

Watch A

Camera A

Car B

Watch B

Camera B

A: Car A is older than Car B.

B: And it's slower. Do you think Car A is quieter?

B PAIR WORK **Which product in each pair do you prefer? Why?**

5 Keep talking!

Go to page 139 for more practice.

B Would you take $10?

1 Interactions Bargaining

A Do you ever bargain for lower prices? Where? For what? Do you enjoy bargaining?

B 🎧 Listen to the conversation. Does Eve buy the lamp? Then practice the conversation.

Eve	Excuse me. How much is this lamp?		Rob	No, I'm sorry. $20 is a good price.
Rob	Oh, it's only $20.		Eve	Well, thanks anyway.
Eve	Wow, that's expensive! How about $10?		Rob	Wait! You can have it for $15.
			Eve	$15? OK. I'll take it.

C 🎧 Listen to the expressions. Then practice the conversation again with the new expressions.

Bargaining for a lower price

> How about . . . ?

> Will you take . . . ?

> Would you take . . . ?

Suggesting a different price

> You can have it / them for . . .

> I'll let you have it / them for . . .

> I'll give it / them to you for . . .

D Number the sentences from 1 to 7. Then practice with a partner.

_____ **A** I'll take them. Thank you very much.

_____ **A** $30? That's pretty expensive. Would you take $20?

_____ **A** OK. Well, thank you anyway.

_____ **A** Excuse me. How much are these earrings?

_____ **B** Just a moment. I'll give them to you for $25.

_____ **B** No, I'm sorry. $30 is the price.

_____ **B** They're only $30.

2 Pronunciation Linked sounds

A 🎧 Listen and repeat. Notice how final consonant sounds are often linked to the vowel sounds that follow them.

How much is this lamp?   It's only $20.

B 🎧 Listen and mark the linked sounds. Then practice with a partner.

1   How much are the earrings?   2   Just a moment.   3   Thanks anyway.

3 Listening How much is it?

A 🎧 Listen to four people shopping at a yard sale. Number the pictures from 1 to 4. (There is one extra picture.)

$ _____ $ _____ $ _____ $ _____ $ _____

B 🎧 Listen again. Write the price the buyer and seller agree on.

4 Speaking What a bargain!

A Write the prices on the tags.

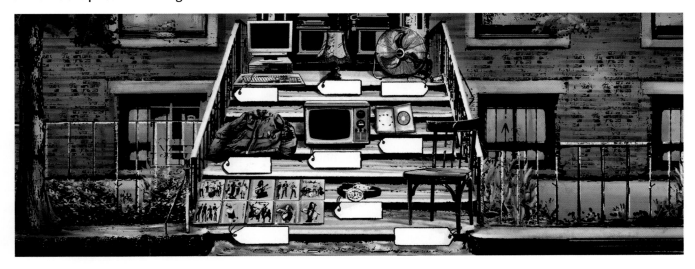

B **PAIR WORK** Role-play the situations. Then change roles.

Student A: Sell the things. You want to sell them for a good price.

Student B: Buy the things. Bargain for lower prices.

A: Excuse me. How much is the computer?

B: It's only $250.

A: That's very expensive. Would you take . . .?

I can bargain. ✓   69

C This hat is too small.

1 Vocabulary Adjectives to describe clothing

A 🎧 Complete the phrases with the correct words. Then listen and check your answers.

baggy	comfortable	pretty	ugly
bright	plain	tight	uncomfortable

1 a _____
shirt

2 _____
jeans

3 _____
shoes

4 a _____
blouse

5 a _____
tie

6 a _____
dress

7 _____
pants

8 an _____
hat

B PAIR WORK Describe your clothing today. Tell your partner.

"I think my shirt is plain, but comfortable. My jeans are a little baggy."

2 Conversation Try it on!

A 🎧 Listen and practice.

Allie Let's look at the jackets.

Paul OK, but I have a class at 3:00. Do we have enough time?

Allie Sure. It's only 1:30. Hey! Look at this black one.

Paul It's cool. Try it on.

Allie OK. What do you think? Does it fit?

Paul No, it's too small. Try this red one.

Allie OK. How does it look? Is it big enough?

Paul I think so. Yeah, it looks good on you.

Allie How much is it? Can you see the tag?

Paul Let's see . . . it's $120.

Allie Oh, no! I only have $60. I don't have enough money.
I can't afford it.

B 🎧 Listen to the rest of the conversation. What else does Allie try on?

3 Grammar 🎧 *Enough* and *too*

Enough *means the right amount.* Too *means more than enough.*

Enough *before nouns*

I have **enough** time.

I don't have **enough** money.

Enough *after adjectives*

The jacket is big **enough**.

The pants aren't long **enough**.

Too *before adjectives*

The jacket is **too** small.

The pants aren't **too** long.

A Complete the sentences with the correct words. Use *too* and *enough*. Then compare with a partner.

big ✓long money uncomfortable

1 How do these pants look? Do you think they're ___long enough___?

2 These shoes look nice, but they're _____. I can't walk at all.

3 Oh, no! I don't have _____. This belt is $30, and I only have $20.

4 The shirt I ordered online is _____. It fits very well.

B Rewrite the sentences. Use *enough* and *too*. Then compare with a partner.

1 Those boots are too small. (enough) — These boots aren't big enough.

2 That belt is $10. I have $10. (enough) _____

3 The jacket is expensive. I can't afford it. (too) _____

4 That belt is $12. I have $10. (enough) _____

5 I wear a large size. This T-shirt isn't big enough. (too) _____

6 These pants aren't long enough. (too) _____

4 Speaking Things I never wear

A Think of your closet at home. Complete the chart with pieces of clothing. Write reasons why you don't wear them.

Things I don't like wearing	Things I never wear
Ties – too ugly	

B GROUP WORK Share your ideas. What do you have in common?

5 Keep talking!

Student A go to page 140 and Student B go to page 144 for more practice.

I can describe how clothing looks and fits. ✓

D A shopper's paradise

1 Reading 🎧

A Read the webpage. Which paragraph includes information about these topics? Number the topics from 1 to 4.

☐ transportation ☐ number of visitors ☐ prices and money ☐ hours

---

CHATUCHAK WEEKEND MARKET

1 With more than 15,000 shops and 200,000 visitors every Saturday and Sunday, Bangkok's Chatuchak Weekend Market is a popular place with visitors to Thailand. You can find plants, flowers, music, jewelry, clothes, food, and even animals!

2 The market is a great place to find bargains, and prices are **generally** low. Most people bargain, but some don't, so don't worry if you don't want to bargain. Just go with a friendly smile and have enough cash in your pocket. There are ATMs for cash, but they are difficult to find, and many **vendors** don't take credit cards. The market is **huge**, and many people walk in circles, even with a map. Don't try to see it all in one day!

3 The market is open from 8:00 to 6:00 Saturday and Sunday. It's good to get there early, before it gets too busy. Wear light, comfortable clothing and bring a bottle of water. And for lunch, try some of Thailand's famous snacks, such as fried scorpions!

4 The market is very easy to get to. It's only a five-minute walk from Mo Chit station on Bangkok's Skytrain. Many people come by train but leave by taxi. It's easier to get your **purchases** back to your hotel that way!

B Read the webpage again. Find the words in **bold**, and check (✓) the correct meaning.

1 **generally** ☐ usually   3 **huge** ☐ easy to find
                ☐ rarely   ☐ very large

2 **vendors** ☐ buyers   4 **purchases** ☐ things you buy
               ☐ sellers   ☐ things you sell

C Check (✓) the tips you think the writer would agree with.

☐ Pay the first price the vendor offers.   ☐ Bring a credit card, not cash.
☐ Arrive in the morning.   ☐ Take the bus home after shopping.

D **PAIR WORK** What would you like about Bangkok's Weekend Market? What wouldn't you like? Tell your partner.

2 Listening Portobello Road Market

A 🎧 **Listen to two friends talk about Portobello Road Market. Answer the questions.**

1 What city is the market in? _____

2 How many days is the outdoor market open? _____

3 When's a good time to visit? _____

4 What's a good way to get there? _____

B 🎧 **Listen again. What can you buy at the market on Saturday? Circle the words you hear.**

animals   cell phones   clothes   fruit   jewelry   meat   vegetables

3 Writing An interesting market

A **Think about a market you know. Answer the questions.**

- What is the name of the market?
- When is it open?
- What can you buy there?
- Where is it?
- When's a good time to visit?

B **Write a description of an interesting market. Use the model and your answers in Part A to help you.**

The Farmers' Market is near my home. It's open every Saturday from 9:00 to 4:00. You can buy the best fruits and vegetables there. A good time to visit is late in the afternoon. It's not too busy then. You don't bargain at this market, but some vendors lower their prices at the end of the day.

C PAIR WORK **Share your writing. How are the markets similar? How are they different?**

4 Speaking A good place to shop

A **Think about things you buy. Add two more things to the list. Then complete the rest of the chart.**

Things I buy	Place	Reason
fruits and vegetables		
shoes		
old furniture		
computers and cell phones		

B GROUP WORK **Share your ideas. Ask and answer questions for more information.**

"I always go to the market to buy fruits and vegetables. They are always fresh, and the people are friendly."

I can discuss good places to shop. ✓

Wrap-up

1 Quick pair review

Lesson A Test your partner!

Say an adjective. Can your partner say its opposite? Take turns. You have one minute.

A: Small.

B: Big.

Lesson B Do you remember?

Complete the conversation with the correct word. You have two minutes.

A   How much is this TV?

B $50

A   Will you _____ $30?
                        1

B   You can _____ it for $45.
                        2

A   How _____ $35?
                3

B   I'll _____ it to you for $40.
                    4

A   OK.

Lesson C Brainstorm!

Make a list of adjectives to describe clothing. Take turns. You and your partner have two minutes.

Lesson D Find out!

What are two things both you and your partner buy at a market? Take turns. You and your partner have two minutes.

A: I buy music at a market. Do you?

B: No, I don't. I buy music online.

2 In the real world

What outdoor markets are famous? Go online and find information in English about an outdoor market. Then write about it.

- What's the name of the market?
- Where is it?
- When is it open?
- What do they sell at the market?

The Otavalo Market
The Otavalo Market is in Ecuador. It's open
every day, but Saturdays are very busy . . . .

8 Fun in the city

Warm Up

A Describe the pictures. What is happening in each picture?

B Which of these things do you like about city life? Which don't you like?

A You shouldn't miss it!

1 Vocabulary Places to see

A 🎧 **Match the words and the pictures. Then listen and check your answers.**

a	botanical garden	c	fountain	e	palace	g	square
b	castle	d	monument	f	pyramid	h	statue

 1
 2
 3
 4

 5
 6
 7
 8

B **PAIR WORK** **Which of the places in Part A do you have where you live? Discuss the places.**

"There's a nice statue in the center of the square."

2 Language in context Attractions in the city

A 🎧 **Read about what to do in these three cities. Which cities are good for shopping?**

Guayaquil, Ecuador
Enjoy shopping, cafés, fountains, and statues on El Malecón, a popular walking area. It's a fantastic place to take a long, slow walk or ride on a tour boat.

Seoul, South Korea
You shouldn't miss the small neighborhood of Insadong. It's a great place to shop for books, pottery, and paintings. Later, you can walk to a nearby palace or relax at an old teahouse.

Cairo, Egypt
Love history? Then you should visit the Egyptian Museum. You can't see it all in one day, so be sure to see King Tut's treasure and the famous "mummy room."

B **What about you? Which city in Part A would you like to visit? Why?**

3 Grammar 🎧 *Should; can*

Should for recommendations	*Can* for possibility

Where **should** I go?
    You **should** visit the Egyptian Museum.
    They **shouldn't** miss Insadong.
    (= They should see Insadong.)
Should she go to Cairo?
    Yes, she **should**.   No, she **shouldn't**.
	What **can** I do there?
	    You **can** enjoy cafés, shops, and fountains.
	    You **can't** see all of the museum in one day.
	Can they take a taxi?
	    Yes, they **can**. No, they **can't**.

Complete the conversation with *should*, *shouldn't*, *can*, or *can't*. Then practice with a partner.

A   _____Should_____ I rent a car in Seoul?

B   No, I think you _____ take the subway. You _____ get around quickly and easily.

A   Oh, good. And what places _____ I visit?

B   Well, you _____ miss the palace, and you _____ also go to the art museum. You _____ see it all in one day because it's very big, but you _____ buy really nice art books and postcards there.

A   OK. Thanks a lot!

4 Listening My city

A **Listen to three people describe their cities. Number the pictures from 1 to 3.**

Istanbul	Mexico City	Florence
1 _____	1 _____	1 _____
2 _____	2 _____	2 _____

B 🎧 **Listen again. Write two things the people say visitors should do in their cities.**

5 Speaking Only one day

A **PAIR WORK** **Imagine these people are planning to visit your town or city for only one day. What places should they visit?**

- a family with teenage children
- two college students
- a businessperson from overseas
- young children on a school trip

"I think the family should visit the town square. They can eat and shop there."

B **GROUP WORK** **Compare your answers from Part A. Do you agree?**

6 Keep talking!

Go to page 142 for more practice.

I can say what people should do in a city. ✓ 77

B I'd recommend going . . .

1 Interactions Recommendations

A Look at the pictures. What do you think the woman is going to do soon?

B 🎧 Listen to the conversation. Was your guess from Part A correct? Then practice the conversation.

Lucy Hi, Alex.	**Alex** I'd recommend going to a samba club.
Alex Oh, hi, Lucy. Are you ready for your trip to Brazil?	**Lucy** A samba club? Really?
Lucy Almost, but I don't really know much about Rio. What would you recommend doing there?	**Alex** Yeah. You can dance or just listen to the music. Everyone has a good time.
	Lucy Great. That sounds fun!

C 🎧 Listen to the expressions. Then practice the conversation again with the new expressions.

Asking for a recommendation

> What would you recommend doing there?

> What would you suggest doing there?

> What do you think I should do there?

Giving a recommendation

> I'd recommend going . . .

> I'd suggest going . . .

> I think you should go . . .

D Put the words in order. Then compare with a partner.

1 you / there / recommend / what / seeing / would _____?

2 I'd / the castle / visiting / suggest _____.

3 the square / I / should / think / you / go to _____.

4 suggest / would / doing / what / you / in Tokyo _____?

5 bus / recommend / I'd / the / taking _____.

78

2 Listening One day in Taipei

🎧 **Listen to Carrie and David get information from the tourist information desk in Taipei. Check (✓) the recommendations you hear.**

1. ☐ I'd suggest visiting Taipei 101.
   ☐ You should visit Taipei 101.
2. ☐ I'd recommend going to the night market.
   ☐ You shouldn't miss the night market.
3. ☐ I'd suggest going to the Fine Arts Museum.
   ☐ I'd recommend going to the Fine Arts Museum.
4. ☐ I think you should take the subway.
   ☐ I'd recommend taking the subway.

3 Speaking Role play

PAIR WORK **Role—play the situation. Then change roles.**

Student A: You are a tourist in London. Ask for recommendations for three things to do.

Student B: You work at a tourist information desk. Give recommendations for three things to do.

TOP LONDON ATTRACTIONS

The British Museum See the famous Rosetta Stone.

The Tate Modern See great art for free.

The London Eye Enjoy views of 55 famous places.

Trafalgar Square Take your picture by the lion statues.

Tower Bridge Walk across the bridge. Fantastic city views!

Buckingham Palace See one of the Royal Family's many homes.

A: Hello. Can I help you?

B: Yes. This is my first time in London. What would you suggest doing here?

A: Well, there are a lot of things to do, but I think you should definitely visit the British Museum. You can see . . .

I can ask for and give a recommendation. ✓

C The best and the worst

1 Vocabulary Adjectives to describe cities

A 🎧 Match the words and pictures. Then listen and check your answers.

| a beautiful | b dangerous | c dirty | d modern | e stressful |

1

2

3

4

5

B 🎧 Write the opposites. Use the words in Part A. Then listen and check your answers.

clean	relaxing	safe	traditional	ugly
dirty				

C PAIR WORK Describe where you live using the words in Parts A and B.

"*Our city is beautiful and clean, but life here can be stressful.*"

2 Conversation Life in Sydney

A 🎧 Listen and practice.

Peter   So, Akemi, how do you like living in Sydney?

Akemi   I miss Japan sometimes, but I love it here. I think it's the most beautiful and one of the most exciting cities in the world.

Peter   But do you find it stressful?

Akemi   Not at all. I know Sydney is the biggest city in Australia, but remember, I'm from Tokyo.

Peter   Oh, yeah. What else do you like about living here?

Akemi   A lot of things. It's very clean and safe. The people are friendly. Oh, and the food here is fantastic.

Peter   I agree. I think Sydney has the best restaurants in the country.

Akemi   Hey, do you want to get something to eat?

Peter   Sure. I know a nice café. It's cheap but good.

B 🎧 Listen to their conversation in the café. How does Akemi describe the café? How does Peter describe the food?

80

3 Grammar 🎧 Superlative adjectives

Sydney is **the biggest** city in Australia.

Sydney is one of **the most exciting** cities in the world.

Sydney has **the best** restaurants in the country.

What is **the cleanest** city in your country?

What city has **the most traditional** restaurants?

Is it the **worst** restaurant?

    Yes, it is.   No, it isn't.

Adjective	Superlative
clean	**the** clean**est**
safe	**the** safe**st**
big	**the** big**gest**
ugly	**the** ugl**iest**
stressful	**the most** stressful
good	**the best**
bad	**the worst**

A Complete the questions with the superlative form of the adjectives. Then compare with a partner.

1 What's one of _____ (old) universities in your country?

2 What's _____ (big) city in your country?

3 What's _____ (modern) city in your country?

4 What's _____ (beautiful) national park?

5 What city has _____ (good) restaurants?

6 What city has _____ (bad) weather?

B Ask and answer the questions in Part A. Discuss your ideas.

University of Cambridge

4 Pronunciation Word stress

A 🎧 Listen and repeat. Notice the stress in the names of these cities.

● ·	· ●	● · ·	· ● ·
Sydney	Ma**drid**	**Can**berra	New **Del**hi

B 🎧 Listen and write the cities in the correct columns in Part A. Then practice with a partner.

    Amsterdam   Berlin   Caracas   Lima

5 Speaking What's the . . . ?

PAIR WORK Ask and answer questions about your town or city.

expensive / hotel	exciting / neighborhood	modern / building
beautiful / park	big / department store	relaxing / place

A: What's the most expensive hotel?

B: I'm not sure it's the most expensive, but the Grand Hotel is very expensive.

6 Keep talking!

Go to page 143 for more practice.

I can make comparisons about my city. ✓

81

D The best place to go

1 Reading 🎧

A Read the message board. Who answers Miguel's question about safety?

Group posts

Topic: Austin or San Antonio?

♡   ◯ 7

miguel Posted May 17 7:06 p.m.
Hi! I live in Mexico and am planning to visit my uncle in Dallas, Texas, next year. I'd also like to visit Austin or San Antonio for a few days. I like the outdoors, local music, good food, friendly people, etc. Are both cities safe? Any other tips appreciated. Thanks! Miguel

rocker Posted May 17 7:23 p.m.
I'm a musician and I live in Austin. I think the music here is the best in Texas. In fact, Austin's nickname is "the Live Music Capital of the World." I can send you the names of some cool music clubs. We have fantastic restaurants here, too.

biker68 Posted May 17 8:54 p.m.
Definitely visit San Antonio. The River Walk is one of the most popular things for visitors to do. There's a lot to do outdoors here, too. And everyone in Texas is friendly. Check out my pics: **myphotos**

susanp Posted May 17 11:09 p.m.
I disagree with rocker. I think the music is better in San Antonio. I've lived in both cities. There is a lot to do outdoors in San Antonio, but there's just more to do in Austin.

richard Posted May 18 6:45 a.m.
Both cities are safe, by the way, so don't worry. I live in Houston. It's the largest city in Texas. You should visit here, too. ☺ Read my travel blog at richard23.cup.org.

traveler Posted May 18 10:31 a.m.
San Antonio has the best food in Texas. Do you like Tex-Mex food? You should go in spring or fall (summer is hot!). I suggest traveling by bus. It's not expensive. Email me with any questions.

miguel Posted May 18 3:22 p.m.
Miguel here again. Thanks, everyone!

B Read the message board again. Answer the questions. Check (✓) your answers.

Who . . .?	rocker	biker68	susanp	richard	traveler
lives in Houston	☐	☐	☐	☐	☐
gives a link to see pictures	☐	☐	☐	☐	☐
writes about the weather	☐	☐	☐	☐	☐
prefers the music in San Antonio	☐	☐	☐	☐	☐
has a travel blog	☐	☐	☐	☐	☐
is a musician	☐	☐	☐	☐	☐

C **PAIR WORK** What do you do when you need advice or a recommendation? Who do you talk to? Tell your partner.

2 Writing A message board

A Choose a topic for a message board. Then write a question asking for a recommendation about your topic. Use the model to help you.

- food
- music
- outdoor activities
- transportation

B GROUP WORK Pass your question to the classmate on your right. Read and answer your classmate's question. Continue to pass, read, and answer all the questions in your group.

C Read the answers to your question. Which recommendation is the best?

> Can you suggest a good restaurant near our school?
> 1. You should go to Mickey's. It's fantastic, but it's expensive.
> 2. I think Thai Palace has the best food.
> 3. I agree. It's the most popular restaurant near here.

3 Speaking The best of the city

A PAIR WORK Complete the chart with information about the best things in your city or town. Give reasons.

The best things about _____	Reasons

A: I think the best thing about our city is the people. They are very friendly and helpful.

B: I agree.

B GROUP WORK Compare your ideas with another pair. Do you agree?

C CLASS ACTIVITY Make a list of all things from Parts A and B. Which is the most popular?

I can discuss aspects of a city. ✓

Wrap-up

1 Quick pair review

Lesson A `Brainstorm!`

Make a list of fun places to see in a city. How many do you know? You have one minute.

Lesson B `Do you remember?`

Check (✓) the questions you can ask when you want a recommendation. You have one minute.

☐ What would you recommend doing there?

☐ Which place is more expensive?

☐ When are you going to China?

☐ What would you suggest doing there?

☐ What are you going to do in Brazil?

☐ What do you think I should do there?

Lesson C `Test your partner!`

Say an adjective to describe a city. Can your partner say the superlative? Take turns. You have one minute.

A: Modern.

B. The most modern.

Lesson D `Guess!`

Describe a city, but don't say its name. Can your partner guess what it is? Take turns. You and your partner have two minutes.

A: It's an old city in Europe. It's beautiful. It has a lot of squares and fountains.

B: Is it Florence?

A: Yes, it is.

2 In the real world

What city would you like to visit? Go to a travel website and find information about the city in English. Then write about it.

● What country is it in?

● What's it like?

● What is there to do in the city?

● What's it famous for?

Montreal
I would like to go to Montreal. It's in Canada.
It's modern and safe . . .

9 People

1
2

a
b

3
4

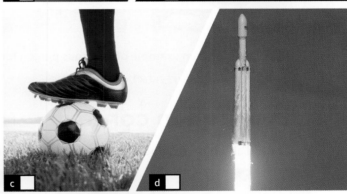
c
d

5
6

e
f

Warm-up

A Match the people and the things they are famous for. Check your answers on page 94.

B Which of the people in Part A would you like to meet? Why?

A Where was he born?

1 Vocabulary Careers

A 🎧 Match the words and the pictures. Then listen and check your answers.

a	astronaut	c	composer	e	director	g	politician
b	athlete	d	designer	f	explorer	h	scientist

1 ☐

2 ☐

3 ☐

4 ☐

5 ☐

6 ☐

7 ☐

8 ☐

B **PAIR WORK** Give an example of a famous person for each category.

"Guillermo del Toro is a famous director."

2 Language in context Famous firsts

A 🎧 Read about these famous firsts. Which famous first happened first?

Emilio Palma was born at Argentina's Esperanza Base in Antarctica in 1978. He was the first person born on the continent.

The first person on the moon in 1969 was American astronaut Neil Armstrong. He was on the moon for only two and a half hours.

Junko Tabei was the first woman to climb Mt. Everest in 1975. She was also the first woman to climb the highest mountains on all seven continents.

Venus and Serena Williams are great athletes. They were the first sisters to win Wimbledon in 2000.

B Which people from Part A would you like to meet? What question would you ask them?

3 Grammar 🎧 *Was / were born*; past of *be*

Where **was** Emilio Palma **born**? He **was born** in Antarctica. He **wasn't born** in Argentina. Where **were** Venus and Serena **born**? They **were born** in the U.S. They **weren't born** in Canada. **Was** he **born** in Antarctica? Yes, he **was**. No, he **wasn't**.	How long **was** Neil Armstrong on the moon? He **was** there for two and a half hours. He **wasn't** there for very long. Where **were** his parents from? They **were** from Argentina. They **weren't** from Antarctica. **Were** they Wimbledon champions in 2000? Yes, they **were**. No, they **weren't**.

A Complete the sentences with the correct past form of *be*. Then compare with a partner.

1 Coco Chanel _____ an amazing French designer.

2 Albert Einstein _____ born in Germany.

3 Alfred Hitchcock _____ a great director.

4 Diego Rivera and Frida Kahlo _____ born in Mexico.

5 Mozart and Beethoven _____ famous composers.

B Correct the false sentences. Then compare with a partner.

1 Ronald Reagan was a British politician. (American)
   He wasn't a British politician. He was an American politician.

2 Zheng He was an early Chinese scientist. (explorer)
   _____

3 Artist Vincent van Gogh was born in the 20th century. (19th century)
   _____

4 Gianni Versace and Yves Saint Laurent were explorers. (designers)
   _____

5 Venus and Serena Williams were born in the late 1970s. (early 1980s)
   _____

4 Speaking Famous people

GROUP WORK Choose a person from the past. Your group asks questions and guesses the person's name. Take turns.

A: He was from Mexico. He was a politician.

B: Is it . . . ?

A: No, sorry. He was born in the 19th century.

C: I think I know. Is it Benito Juárez?

5 Keep talking!

Student A go to page 141 and Student B go to page 145 for more practice.

I can ask and talk about people from the past. ✓

B I'm not sure, but I think . . .

1 Interactions Certainty and uncertainty

A Look at the pictures. Where are the people? What are they doing?

B 🎧 Listen to the conversation. Does Mike know the answer to both questions? Then practice the conversation.

Mike	Let's go over more questions before our test tomorrow.
Jenny	OK. What was the original name of New York City?
Mike	It was New Amsterdam.
Jenny	Are you sure?
Mike	I'm positive.

Jenny	Correct! This one's more difficult. Who was Plato's teacher?
Mike	I'm not sure, but I think it was Aristotle.
Jenny	Actually, Aristotle was Plato's student. Socrates was his teacher.
Mike	Oh, right.

C 🎧 Listen to the expressions. Then practice the conversation again with the new expressions.

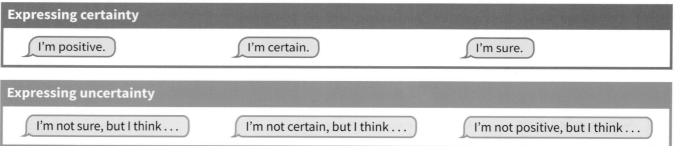

Expressing certainty

I'm positive.   I'm certain.   I'm sure.

Expressing uncertainty

I'm not sure, but I think . . .   I'm not certain, but I think . . .   I'm not positive, but I think . . .

D Circle the answer you think is correct. Practice with a partner and use expressions from Part C. Then check your answers on page 94.

1 Barack Obama was president of the **U.S.** / **U.K.**

2 Mozart was born in the **16**th / **17**th / **18**th century.

3 Neymar da Silva Santos, Jr's first soccer team was **Barcelona** / **Paris Saint-Germain** / **Santos**.

4 Che Guevara was born in **Bolivia** / **Argentina** / **Cuba**.

5 The 2016 Olympics were in **Sochi** / **Rio** / **Sydney**.

A: Barack Obama was the president of the U.S.

B: Are you sure?

A: I'm positive.

2 Listening Sorry, that's not right.

A Do you know the answers to these questions? Write your guesses in the first column.

		Your guess	Player's guess	
1	Where were the 2016 Olympics?			☐
2	Who was the winner of the 2014 World Cup?			☐
3	In what century was Pablo Picasso born?			☐
4	Who was the author of the play *Hamlet*?			☐
5	How long was Barack Obama president of the U.S.?			☐

B 🎧 Listen to four friends play a board game. Write the players' guesses in the second column.

C 🎧 Listen again. Check (✓) the players' guesses that are correct.

3 Speaking Do you know?

A **PAIR WORK** Look at the pictures and the categories. Add another category. Then write two questions for each category. Be sure you know the answers!

Actors and actresses

_____

_____

_____

Athletes

_____

_____

_____

Singers and musicians

_____

_____

_____

_____

_____

_____

B **GROUP WORK** Ask your questions. Use expressions of certainty or uncertainty in the answers.

A: Where was Brad Pitt born?

B: I'm not sure, but I think he was born in . . .

A: How old is he?

I can express certainty and uncertainty. ✓

C People I admire

1 Vocabulary Personality adjectives

A 🎧 Match the words in the paragraphs and the definitions. Then listen and check your answers.

I admire U.S. President Abraham Lincoln. He was **honest**[1] as a lawyer and often worked for free. He was **brave**[2] and kept the country together during war. He was a very **inspiring**[3] person.

–Jin Ju

Nobel Prize in Literature winner Kazuo Ishiguro is very **passionate**[4] about his writing. He's very **intelligent**[5], and I really admire his novels.

–Celia

Bono is a **talented**[6] musician, but he's also a **caring**[7] person. I admire him for his fight against world poverty. He's very **determined**[8], and he's helping a lot of poor people.

–Mark

_____ very good at something
__1__ open, telling the truth
_____ not afraid of anything
_____ nice to other people

_____ making other people want to do something
_____ able to understand things quickly and easily
_____ trying everything possible to do something
_____ showing a strong feeling about something

B **PAIR WORK** What other personality adjectives can you think of? Discuss your ideas.

2 Conversation I really admire him.

A 🎧 Listen and practice.

Paul   Did you finish your report, Emma?

Emma   Yeah, I did. I finished it two days ago.

Paul   Good for you! So who did you write about?

Emma   Jacques Cousteau. I really admire him.

Paul   I don't think I know him. What did he do?

Emma   A lot! He was a French scientist and explorer. He loved nature and studied the sea. He made documentaries and wrote books about the world's oceans. He won a lot of prizes for his work.

Paul   Wow! He sounds like an inspiring guy.

Emma   He was. He was really passionate about his work.

B 🎧 Listen to the rest of the conversation. When did Jacques Cousteau die?

3 Grammar 🎧 Simple past; *ago*

Who **did** you **write** about?
I **wrote** about Jacques Cousteau.
I **didn't write** about his son.
What **did** he **do**?
He **made** documentaries.
Did you **finish** your report?
Yes, I **did**.   No, I **didn't**.

Period of time + *ago*
I finished the report **two days ago**.
I researched it **a week ago**.
I saw a documentary **four years ago**.
He died **a long time ago**.

A Complete the conversation with the simple past form of the verbs. Then practice with a partner.

A Why _____ you _____ (decide) to write about Serena Williams for your report?

B Well, I _____ (want) to write about an athlete. And I think she's very inspiring. In 2008, she _____ (start) the Serena Williams Foundation. It builds schools. Then in 2010, she _____ (write) the book *My Life: Queen of the Court*.

A What else did she do?

B Well, in 2016, she _____ (dance) in her friend Beyoncé's video. In September 2017, she _____ (have) a baby girl!

B PAIR WORK Ask and answer questions about when Serena Williams did these things. Use *ago* in the answers.

have a baby	dance in a video	start a foundation	write a book

4 Pronunciation Simple past *-ed* endings

🎧 Listen and repeat. Notice the different ways the past simple endings are pronounced.

/t/		/d/		/id/	
finished	asked	played	admired	wanted	created

5 Speaking What did they do?

GROUP WORK Use the adjectives to describe people you know. What did the people do?

brave	caring	honest	intelligent	talented

"My sister Megumi is very brave. She traveled alone in Canada and . . ."

6 Keep Talking

Go to page 146 for more practice.

I can describe people I admire. ✓

D Making a difference

1 Reading

A Read the biography. How did Dr. Muhammad Yunus make a difference?

   a He won the Nobel Peace Prize.   **b** He helped the poor.   **c** He studied economics.

A DIFFERENT KIND OF BANKER

Dr. Muhammad Yunus, a banker and economist, was born in Bangladesh in 1940. He studied economics at Dhaka University in Bangladesh. He taught for a few years and then went to the United States to continue his studies. He returned home to Bangladesh in 1972 and started teaching again.

One day in 1976, Yunus visited a poor **village** in his home country. There he met some women who wanted to make furniture, but they didn't have enough money. He decided to help them and gave them $27 of his own money.

They made and sold the furniture, **made a profit**, and then returned the money to Dr. Yunus. At that point, he saw how very little money could help a lot. He decided to help poor people. A bank **loaned** him the money. In 1983, Yunus started Grameen Bank. This bank loans money to poor people. Dr. Yunus and Grameen Bank received the 2006 Nobel Peace Prize for their work with the poor.

In 2009, the bank had 7.95 million customers, and 97% of these customers were women. The success of the bank inspired other people in many different countries to start similar banks. Yunus once said, "**Conventional** banks look for the rich; we look for the absolutely poor."

B Number these events from Dr. Yunus's life from 1 to 8.

_____ He returned to Bangladesh.   _____ He studied at Dhaka University.

_____ He was born in 1940.   _____ He gave money to some women in 1976.

_____ He started the Grameen Bank.   _____ He won the Nobel Peace Prize.

_____ He studied in the United States.   _____ He inspired other people.

C Read the biography again. Find the words in **bold**, and check (✓) the correct meaning.

1 A **village** is:

   ☐ a very small town   ☐ a big place where a lot of people live

2 If you **made a profit**, you:

   ☐ lost money   ☐ made money

3 If someone **loaned** you money, you:

   ☐ gave back the money   ☐ kept the money

4 A **conventional** bank is:

   ☐ usual   ☐ unusual

D **PAIR WORK** How would you describe Dr. Yunus? Tell your partner.

2 Writing A biography

A **PAIR WORK** Discuss famous people who made a big difference in people's lives. Answer the questions.

- What are their names?
- What do you know about their lives?
- What did they do?
- How did they make a difference?

B Write a short biography about a famous person who made a difference. Use the model and the answers in Part A to help you.

José Antonio Abreu
José Antonio Abreu is a Venezuelan economist. He is also a talented musician. In 1975, he started a music school for poor children. He wanted to help these children and was determined to change their lives with music. Today, children all over Venezuela are playing in orchestras.

C **GROUP WORK** Share your writing. Who do you think made the biggest difference?

3 Listening Life lessons

A 🎧 Listen to three people describe the people who made a difference in their lives. Check (✓) the qualities they use to describe those people.

	Qualities		What did the people teach them?
1	☐ caring ☐ talented	☐ intelligent ☐ creative	a. how to sing b. to be a musician
2	☐ brave ☐ honest	☐ generous ☐ determined	a. never to quit b. how to play soccer
3	☐ determined ☐ caring	☐ honest ☐ inspiring	a. how to teach English b. the qualities of a good teacher

B 🎧 Listen again. What did the people teach them? Circle the correct answers.

4 Speaking In my life

GROUP WORK Tell your group about a person who made a difference in your life. Use the questions below and your own ideas.

- How do you know this person?
- What did he or she teach you?
- What did he or she do?
- How would you describe him or her?

A: My aunt made a difference in my life.

B: Oh, yeah? Why?

A: She taught me to think of other people.

I can describe people who made a difference. ✓

Wrap-up

1 Quick pair review

Lesson A `Brainstorm!`

Make a list of careers. How many do you know? You have two minutes.

Lesson B `Guess!`

Say the name of a famous person. Does your partner know where he or she was born?
Take turns. You have two minutes.

A: Albert Einstein.

B: He was born in Germany.

A: Are you sure?

B: I'm positive.

B: Oprah Winfrey.

A: I'm not sure, but I think she was born in Mississippi.

Lesson C `Test your partner!`

Say six verbs. Can your partner write the simple past form of the verbs correctly?
Check his or her answers. Take turns. You and your partner have two minutes.

1 _____   3 _____   5 _____

2 _____   4 _____   6 _____

Lesson D `Find out!`

Who are two people both you and your partner think made a difference in the world?
What qualities do they have? Take turns. You and your partner have two minutes.

A: I think Nelson Mandela made a difference.

B: Me, too. He was determined and inspiring.

A: Yes, he was.

2 In the real world

Who do you admire? Go online and find five things that he or she did
that you think are interesting. Then write about this person.

Sheryl Sandberg
I admire Sheryl Sandberg. She is the Chief
Operating Officer of Facebook. She's a great
businessperson. She also helps a lot of women
and children . . .

10 In a restaurant

LESSON A	**LESSON B**	**LESSON C**	**LESSON D**
● Menu items ● Articles	● Ordering food ● Checking information	● Interesting food ● Present perfect for experience	● Reading: "Restaurants with a Difference" ● Writing: A review

Warm Up

A What kinds of food do you think each place serves?

B Check (✓) the top three places you would like to try. Why?

A The ice cream is fantastic!

1 Vocabulary Menu items

A 🎧 Label the menu with the correct words. Then listen and check your answers.

Appetizers	Desserts	Main dishes	Side dishes

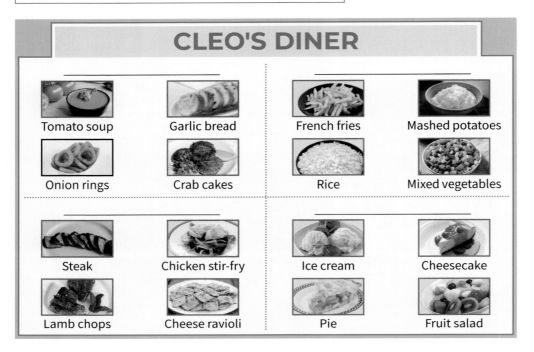

CLEO'S DINER

Tomato soup   Garlic bread   French fries   Mashed potatoes

Onion rings   Crab cakes   Rice   Mixed vegetables

Steak   Chicken stir-fry   Ice cream   Cheesecake

Lamb chops   Cheese ravioli   Pie   Fruit salad

B PAIR WORK Give an example of another menu item for each category.

"Another example of a main dish is spaghetti with meatballs. Another side dish . . ."

2 Language in context Any recommendations?

A 🎧 Listen to Jeff chat with his friends online. Who recommends the ice cream?

Jeff I'm thinking of eating out tonight. Any recommendations?

Junko I'd recommend going to Cleo's Diner. They have great food and good service.

Tony12 Yeah, Cleo's is amazing. Get an appetizer there. They're excellent.

Jeff GR8! How are the main dishes?

Tony12 I had steak with some French fries. The steak was great, but the fries weren't.

Junko You should try a dessert there, too. The ice cream is fantastic!

Jeff I love ice cream! THX. ☺ Does anyone want to join me?

B What about you? What do you do when you need a recommendation for a restaurant?

3 Grammar 🎧 Articles

Use a / an *to talk about nonspecific singular count nouns* Try **a** dessert. Get **an** appetizer. Use some *before plural count and noncount nouns.* Let's order **some** French fries. Let's order **some** garlic bread.	Use the *to talk about specific count and noncount nouns.* I had **the** crab cakes. **The** ice cream is fantastic. Use the *to name count and noncount nouns a second time.* I had a steak and some French fries. **The** steak was great, but **the** fries weren't.

Circle the words. Then compare with a partner.

A I'm glad we came here. It's a great place.

B So, do you want to share **an / some** appetizer?

A Sure. How about **an / the** onion rings?

B Perfect!

A And do you want to get **a / some** crab cakes?

B I don't think so. I'm not *that* hungry.

A I'm going to get **a / the** lamb chops with **a / some** rice.

B I think I want **a / the** steak. I heard it's delicious.

A **A / The** desserts are good. I love **an / the** ice cream.

B Yeah, we should order **a / an** dessert later.

A Let's find **the / some** waiter. Where is he?

4 Pronunciation *The* before vowel and consonant sounds

A 🎧 **Listen and repeat. Notice how *the* is pronounced before vowel and consonant sounds.**

/i/		
the **a**ppetizer	the **i**ce cream	the **o**range

/ə/		
the **l**amb	the **f**ruit	the **p**ie

B PAIR WORK **Practice the conversation in Exercise 3.**

5 Speaking What to order?

A PAIR WORK **Do you usually order an appetizer, a main dish, a side dish, and a dessert in restaurants? Discuss your ideas.**

A: I usually order a main dish and a side dish. I don't really like desserts.

B: I sometimes order an appetizer, but I always order a dessert.

B PAIR WORK **Look at the menu in Exercise 1. What would you order?**

"The chicken stir-fry and the rice look good. I'd order that."

6 Keep talking!

Go to page 147 for more practice.

I can talk about menus and eating out. ✓

B I'll have the fish, please.

1 Interactions At a restaurant

A When was the last time you went to a restaurant? Who did you go with? What did you order?

B 🎧 Listen to the conversation. What does Maria order? Then practice the conversation.

Waiter	Are you ready to order?	**Maria**	No, I don't think so.
Maria	Yes, I think so.	**Waiter**	All right. Let me check that. You'd like the fish, with rice, and a small salad.
Waiter	What would you like?		
Maria	I'll have the fish with some rice, and a small salad, please.	**Maria**	Yes, that's right.
		Waiter	Would you like some water?
Waiter	Anything else?	**Maria**	Sure, that would be great. Thank you.

C 🎧 Listen to the expressions. Then practice the conversation again with the new expressions.

Ordering food

> I'll have . . ., please.   I'd like . . ., please.   Can I have . . .,please?

Checking information

> Let me check that.   Let me read that back.   Let me repeat that.

D PAIR WORK Have conversations like the one in Part B. Use the food below.

2 **Listening** Food orders

A 🎧 **Listen to people order food. How many people order dessert? Circle the correct answer.**

one   two   three

B 🎧 **Listen again. Correct any wrong information on these orders.**

1

Mickey's 🍒

chicken

rice

mixed vegetables

apple pie

2

Mickey's 🍒

crab cakes

lamb chops

French fries

small salad

water

chocolate cake

medium mushroom pizza

iced tea

3 **Speaking** Role play

PAIR WORK **Role-play the situation. Then change roles.**

Student A: You are waiter or waitress at Puck's Place. Greet the customer, take his or her order, and then check the information.

Student B: You are a customer at Puck's Place. Order from the menu.

✧PUCK'S PLACE✧

✧PUCK'S PLACE✧

Appetizers
Chicken salad • Pasta salad • Onion soup
Chicken soup • Crab cakes • Garlic bread

Main dishes
Lamb chops • Steak
Chicken stir-fry • Fish • Cheese ravioli

Sides
French fries • Rice
Mixed vegetables • Mashed potatoes

Desserts
Apple pie • Chocolate ice cream • Fruit salad

Drinks
Tea • Coffee • Lemonade • Soda

A: Hello. Are you ready to order?

B: Yes. I'll have the onion soup. And can I have the fish and some white rice, please? Also, . . .

I can order food in a restaurant. ✓

99

C Have you ever . . .?

1 Vocabulary Interesting food

A 🎧 Complete the chart with the correct words. Then listen and check your answers.

avocados   blue cheese   carrot juice   dates   frozen yogurt

oysters   plantains   seaweed   soy milk   squid

Dairy	Seafood	Fruits / Vegetables	Drinks

B **PAIR WORK** Which food in Part A do you like? do you dislike? would you like to try? Tell your partner.

"I like oysters. I don't like carrot juice. I'd like to try squid."

2 Conversation Dinner plans

A 🎧 Listen and practice.

Ellen   What are you doing tonight?

Peter   I'm going to World Café with my brother. Have you ever been there?

Ellen   No, I haven't. But I heard it's good.

Peter   I looked at their menu online this morning. They serve some really interesting food.

Ellen   Oh, yeah? Like what?

Peter   Fresh oysters. I've never had oysters, so I want to try them. Have you ever eaten them?

Ellen   Yeah, I have. I think they're delicious.

Peter   I've had squid. Are they similar?

Ellen   Um, not really. Do they only serve seafood?

Peter   No, they serve a little of everything.

B 🎧 Listen to Peter's message to Ellen the next day. What food did he like?

3 Grammar 🎧 Present perfect for experience

I've **been** to World Café.	I **haven't tried** the desserts.
I've **had** squid.	I've never **eaten** oysters.

Have you **ever been** to World Café?

Yes, I **have.**   No, I **haven't.**

Contractions   I've = I have   I haven't = I have not.

Past participles

be	**been**
drink	**drunk**
eat	**eaten**
have	**had**
try	**tried**

A Complete the conversations with the present perfect form of the verbs. Then practice with a partner.

1 A This place looks fun. I _____ (never / be) here.

B I love it here. I _____ (be) here many times.

A Everything looks delicious.

B _____ you _____ (ever / eat) Mexican food before?

A I _____ (have) tacos, but I'd like to try something new.

2 A I _____ (never / try) frozen yogurt. Can you recommend a flavor?

B I _____ (have) most flavors, and they're all good.

A _____ you _____ (ever / try) the green tea flavor?

B No, I _____ (have / not), but you should try it!

B Make sentences about your food experiences.

1 be / to a Turkish restaurant _____

2 eat / oysters _____

3 drink / soy milk _____

4 have / plantains _____

5 try / blue cheese _____

C PAIR WORK Ask *Have you ever . . .?* questions about the experiences in Part B.

4 Speaking Food experiences

A Add two more food experiences to the list.

eat / dates	have / seaweed	_____ / _____
try / Vietnamese food	drink / carrot juice	_____ / _____

B PAIR WORK Discuss your experiences. What food would you like to try?

A: Have you ever tried Vietnamese food?

B: Yes, I have. It's delicious.

5 Keep talking!

Go to page 148 for more practice.

I can ask about and describe food experiences. ✓

D Restaurant experiences

1 Reading 🎧

A 🎧 **Read the web page. Which sentence describes all three restaurants? Check (✓) the correct answer.**

☐ They don't have a lot of light.　　☐ They are in good locations.

☐ They're not very expensive.　　☐ They are very unusual.

RESTAURANTS WITH A DIFFERENCE

Ninja Akasaka is a popular restaurant in Tokyo. A ninja in dark clothes greets guests at the door and takes them through the dark hallways of the ninja house to their tables. The waiters also dress as ninjas. Ninja Akasaka has over a hundred delicious dishes to choose from. There's also a branch of the restaurant in Manhattan – Ninja New York.

♡ ◯ 95 likes   Follow

Annalakshmi is a vegetarian restaurant in Chennai, India, with additional restaurants in three other countries. There are no prices on the menu, so guests pay what they can! The people who work there are volunteers and take turns serving customers, cleaning tables, and washing dishes. Indian art covers the walls, and there are even live music and dance performances.

♡ ◯ 78 likes   Follow

At ***Dans Le Noir*** (In the Dark) in Paris, guests order their food in a place with a lot of light, but then they eat in darkness. They focus on the touch, smell, and taste of the food. The waiters there are blind, so when guests are ready to leave, they call the waiter's name. Their waiter then takes them back to the place where they ordered the food. There are additional restaurants in London and Moscow.

♡ ◯ 64 likes   Follow

B **Read the web page again. Write T (true), F (false), or NI (no information) next to the sentences.**

1　Guests dress as ninjas at Ninja Akasaka. _____

2　Ninja New York is more popular than Ninja Akasaka. _____

3　Annalakshmi has restaurants in four countries. _____

4　Every guest at Annalakshmi pays the same price. _____

5　Guests never see their food at Dans Le Noir. _____

6　The cooks at Dans Le Noir are blind. _____

C **PAIR WORK** **Which restaurants in Part A do you think you'd enjoy? Why? Have you ever been to an unusual restaurant? Tell your partner.**

2 Listening So, what did you think?

A 🎧 Listen to three couples talk about the restaurants in Exercise 1. Where did each couple eat?
Number the restaurants from 1 to 3.

☐ Ninja Akasaka ☐ Annalakshmi ☐ Dans Le Noir

B 🎧 Listen again. Check (✓) the things each couple liked about the experience.

	the service	the prices	the location	the food
1	☐	☐	☐	☐
2	☐	☐	☐	☐
3	☐	☐	☐	☐

3 Writing A review

A Think of a restaurant you like. Answer the questions.

- What is the name of the restaurant?
- What type of food does it serve?
- When were you there last?
- What would you recommend ordering?
- What do you like about the restaurant?

B Write a short review of your favorite restaurant. Use the model and your answers from Part A to help you.

> My Favorite Restaurant
> Seoul Barbecue is my favorite restaurant. It serves delicious, healthy
> Korean food. I went there last week and loved it. I ordered beef, and
> I had some small side dishes. I would recommend doing that. It's fun
> because you cook your own meat at the table. It's a little expensive,
> but I really liked the service. I'd recommend this restaurant.

C **CLASS ACTIVITY** Post your reviews around the room. Read your classmates' reviews. Then get more information about the restaurant that interests you the most.

4 Speaking Restaurant recommendations

PAIR WORK Recommend a good place to go for each situation. Discuss your ideas.

- take an overseas visitor
- meet a big group of friends
- have a child's birthday party
- have a quiet dinner for two
- get a quick, cheap lunch
- enjoy live music

A: What's a good place to meet a big group of friends?
B: How about . . .? There's a private room for big groups.

Wrap-up

1 Quick pair review

Lesson A Brainstorm!

Make a list of menu items. How many do you know? You have two minutes.

Lesson B Do you remember?

Check (✓) the things you can say to order food. You have one minute.

☐ I'll have some French fries, please.

☐ Try the cheesecake, please.

☐ What would you like?

☐ Can I have the steak, please?

☐ Let me check that.

☐ I'd like some pie, please.

Lesson C Find out!

What interesting food have you and your partner both tried? Take turns. You and your partner have two minutes.

A: I've eaten squid.

B: I haven't. I've eaten . . .

Lesson D Guess!

Describe a restaurant in your city, but don't say its name. Can your partner guess which one it is? Take turns. You and your partner have two minutes.

A: This restaurant is on Main Street. It has good seafood, and the food is cheap. The service is fantastic.

B: Is it Big Fish?

A: Yes, it is.

2 In the real world

What would you like to order? Go online and find a menu for a restaurant in English. Then write about it.

- What is the name of the restaurant?
- What appetizers, main dish, and side dishes would you like to order?
- What drink would you like to try?
- What dessert would you like to eat?

Alphabet Café
I'd like to eat at Alphabet Café. I'd like
some garlic bread and the spaghetti . . .

11 Entertainment

Warm Up

A Match the words and the pictures.

_____ an amusement park   _____ a dance performance   _____ a play

_____ a concert   _____ a movie   _____ a soccer game

B Which of these types of entertainment do you want to go to? Rank them from 1 (really want to go) to 6 (don't really want to go).

A   I'm not a fan of dramas.

1 Vocabulary Types of movies

A 🎧 **Match the types of movies and the pictures. Then listen and check your answers.**

a	an action movie	c	a comedy	e	a horror movie	g	a science fiction movie
b	an animated movie	d	a drama	f	a musical	h	a western

1 [g]

2 [d]

3 ☐

4 ☐

5 ☐

6 ☐

7 ☐

8 ☐

B **PAIR WORK** **What are your favorite types of movies? Give an example of the types you like. Tell your partner.**

"I love action movies and dramas. My favorite movies are . . ."

2 Language in context At the movies

A 🎧 **Listen to two friends at the movies. What type of movie are they watching?**

B **What about you? Are you ever late for movies? Do you like to sit in the front, middle, or back?**

3 Grammar 🎧 *So, too, either,* and *neither*

I'm a fan of science fiction movies.
    So am I / I am, **too**.
    Oh, I'm not. I like comedies.
 	
I like to sit in the front row.
    So do I. / I do, **too**.
    Really? I don't. I prefer the back row.
	I'm not usually late for movies.
	    Neither am I. / I'm not, **either**.
	    Oh, I am. I'm always late.
	
	I don't buy popcorn.
	    Neither do I. / I don't, **either**.
	    Oh, I do. And I always get a soda.

A Respond to the sentences in two different ways. Use *so, too, either,* or *neither*. **Compare with a partner.**

1 I'm not a fan of dramas.   _Neither am I._   _I'm not, either._

2 I love animated movies.   _____   _____

3 I'm not interested in action movies.   _____   _____

4 I'm interested in old westerns.   _____   _____

5 I don't watch horror movies.   _____   _____

6 I don't like science fiction movies.   _____   _____

B **PAIR WORK** **Make the sentences in Part A true for you. Respond with** *so, too, either,* **or** *neither*.

A: I'm not a fan of dramas.

B: Neither am I.   **OR**   Really? I am. My favorite drama is . . .

4 Speaking Movie talk

A **Complete the sentences with true information.**

I like to eat _____candy_____ at the movies.
            (snack)

I really like _____ .
    (actor or actress)

I'm not a fan of _____ .
      (actor or actress)

I want to see _____ .
    (name of movie)

I don't really want to see _____ .
      (name of movie)

I often see movies at _____ .
    (name of theater)

I usually see movies with _____ .
      (name of person)

B **PAIR WORK** **Take turns reading your sentences. Respond appropriately.**

A: I like to eat candy at the movies.

B: I don't. I like to eat popcorn.

C **GROUP WORK** **What movies are playing right now? Which ones do you want to see?**
Can you agree on a movie to see together?

5 Keep talking!

Go to page 149 for more practice.

I can talk about my movie habits and opinions. ✓

B Any suggestions?

1 Interactions Suggestions

A What do you like to do on weekends? Who do you usually spend weekends with? How do you decide what to do?

B 🎧 Listen to the conversation. What do they decide to do on the weekend? Then practice the conversation.

Douglas What do you want to do this weekend?	**Jocelyn** I hate karaoke, and we went to the movies last week.
Jocelyn I don't really know. Do you have any suggestions?	**Douglas** Let's go to the food festival.
Douglas Well, there's an outdoor movie in the park, a food festival, and a karaoke contest.	**Jocelyn** OK. That sounds good. Have you ever been to one?
	Douglas No, but it sounds like a lot of fun.

C 🎧 Listen to the expressions. Then practice the conversation again with the new expressions.

Asking for suggestions

> Do you have any suggestions?   What do you suggest?   Any suggestions?

Giving a suggestion

> Let's . . .   Why don't we . . . ?   We could . . .

D Number the sentences from 1 to 8. Then practice with a partner.

_____ **A** A play? That's not a bad idea.

_____ **A** I'm not sure. We could see a movie.

___1___ **A** Let's do something different tonight.

_____ **A** Why don't we see the comedy?

_____ **B** We always see movies. Why don't we see a play?

_____ **B** OK. And let's have dinner before.

_____ **B** There are two plays. One is a drama, the other a comedy.

___2___ **B** OK. What do you suggest?

2 **Listening** Let's get together!

A 🎧 Listen to three conversations. Check (✓) what the people decide to do.

	What they decide to do		Place	Time
1	☐ go to a movie	☐ watch a movie at home		
2	☐ go out to eat	☐ order take-out food		
3	☐ go to a play	☐ go to a baseball game		

B 🎧 Listen again. Where and when are they going to meet? Write the place and time.

3 **Speaking** This weekend

A PAIR WORK Complete the chart with what is happening this weekend where you live.

	Movies	Music	Sports	Festivals
Friday				
Saturday				
Sunday				

B PAIR WORK Work with a new partner. Look at your charts. Decide to do three things together.

A: Let's do something fun this weekend.

B: All right. Any suggestions?

A: Well, we could see the new horror movie. Do you like horror movies?

B: No, I don't. Sorry. Why don't we . . . ?

I can ask for and give suggestions. ✓

C All of us love music.

1 Vocabulary Types of music

A 🎧 **Listen to the song clips. Number the types of music you hear from 1 to 10. Then check your answers.**

pop

rock

jazz

country

classical

folk

hip-hop

techno

reggae

blues

B **PAIR WORK** **Say the name of a musician for each type of music in Part A. Tell your partner.**

"Jennifer Lopez sings pop music."

2 Conversation A music recital

A 🎧 **Listen and practice.**

Ingrid	These kids are great musicians. Do all of the students at this school learn a musical instrument?
John	No, I don't think so, but most of them do.
Ingrid	I see. And do most of the schools in this city have bands?
John	I'm not sure. I know a lot of them around here do. Some of the schools even have their own jazz bands.
Ingrid	How interesting! Do you know what's next?
John	I think there's going to be a violin solo.

B 🎧 **Listen to their conversation after the recital. What type of music do the children prefer to play?**

3 Grammar 🎧 Determiners

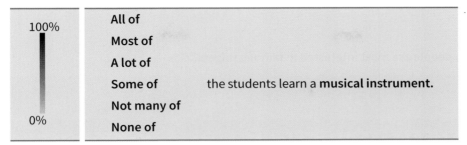

100% 0%	All of Most of A lot of Some of the students learn a **musical instrument.** Not many of None of

A Look at the picture of the Branson family. Complete the sentences with determiners. Then compare with a partner.

1 _____ of them are singing.

2 _____ of them have costumes.

3 _____ of them are sitting.

4 _____ of them are playing an instrument.

5 _____ of them have blond hair.

6 _____ of them are dancing.

B Make true sentences using determiners. Tell your partner.

1 . . . of my favorite songs are pop songs.

2 . . . of my friends play an instrument.

3 . . . of my classmates play in rock bands.

4 . . . of my friends enjoy singing karaoke.

4 Pronunciation Reduction of *of*

A 🎧 Listen and repeat. Notice how *of* is sometimes pronounced /ə/ before consonant sounds.

/ə/	/ə/	/ə/
All of the students	A lot of the schools	None of my friends

B PAIR WORK Practice the sentences in Exercise 3A. Reduce *of* to /ə/.

5 Speaking Ask the class.

A CLASS ACTIVITY Add a type of music, a song, or a singer to the question.
Then ask your classmates the question.
Write the number of people who answer "yes."

Do you like _____ ? ☐

B Share your information. Use determiners.

"Some of us like hip-hop."

6 Keep talking!

Go to page 150 for more practice.

I can report the results of a survey. ✓

111

D Singing shows around the world

1 Reading 🎧

A Read the online article. Which people are most interested in famous singers?

EVERYBODY LOVES A SING-OFF

Every year, thousands of people around the world enter singing competitions on TV, and millions of people watch to see who wins. Why do we love these programs so much?

Kanda, Thailand
Favorite show: The Mask Singer
"I'm a fan because I like seeing regular people become famous. Everybody loves a rags-to-riches story, right? I really enjoy shows where you choose favorites and watch them improve each week. Also, I love when I can vote for a singer – it's fun to help decide who will be the next big star!"

♡ ◯ 34 likes   Follow

Andrew, USA
Favorite show: American Idol
"I usually watch singing competitions because I want to see singers before they are stars. Did you know that singers like Justin Timberlake, Beyoncé, and One Direction were all on TV competitions? Not many of the competitors will become famous – but sometimes, I hear a singer and I just know she's going to be great."

♡ ◯ 57 likes   Follow

Eduardo, Chile
Favorite show: Festival Internacional de la Canción de Viña del Mar
"Everybody likes to sing – that's why these competitions are so popular. All of my friends sing in the shower, in the car, walking down the street. But I wish it wasn't all pop music. How about a hip-hop competition? Or a techno contest with DJs? That would be really cool."

♡ ◯ 48 likes   Follow

Wiktoria, Poland
Favorite show: Eurovision
"I like to watch people sing badly. Seriously, I can hear good singing any time on the radio — it's more fun to hear people who aren't so good. I like to see what happens when people get on stage with a big audience. Will they perform well? Or will they miss a beat? That's really why most of us watch – we like to be the judge."

♡ ◯ 45 likes   Follow

B Read the article again. Answer the questions.

1 Why does Kanda watch singing shows? _____

2 What does Andrew want to see? _____

3 What does Yandri not like about competitions? _____

4 Why does Wiktoria like to see people sing badly? _____

C GROUP WORK Do you like to watch singing competitions? Why or why not? Would you enter a competition? What kind of music would you sing? Discuss your ideas.

112

2 Listening Classical music hour

A 🎧 **Listen to a radio host talk about the musician Lang Lang. Where is Lang Lang from?**

B 🎧 **Listen again. Check (✓) the correct answers.**

1 1. Lang Lang had his first music lessons at age:

☐ three ☐ five

2 He received his first award at age:

☐ five ☐ fifteen

3 He likes to share music with:

☐ young people ☐ older people

4 He also works with:

☐ UNICEF ☐ United Nations University

5 Besides classical music he loves:

☐ jazz and rock ☐ jazz, hip-hop, and pop

3 Writing A popular musician

A **Think of your favorite musician or a popular musician. Answer the questions.**

- Where is this person from?
- What type of music is this person famous for?
- What is this person's best song?
- What is interesting about this person?

B **Write a short description about the musician. Use the model and your answers from Part A to help you.**

My Favorite Singer
My favorite singer is Thalia. She's from Mexico. She sings different types
of music, but mostly she sings pop and dance music. My favorite song is
"No, No, No." She records songs in many languages. She sings in English,
Spanish, French, and Tagalog.

C GROUP WORK **Share your writing. Did any of you write about the same musician?**

4 Speaking Make a playlist

A PAIR WORK **Make a list of the most important singers, bands, or musicians from your country. What are their most popular songs?**

B PAIR WORK **Create a five-track playlist. Use your notes.**

A: I think . . . is very important.

B: So do I. A lot of young people like his music.

C GROUP WORK **Present your playlist and explain your choices. Ask and answer questions to get more information.**

I can describe important singers and musicians. ✓

Wrap-up

1 Quick pair review

Lesson A `Find out!`
What are two types of movies that both you and your partner like? You have two minutes.

A: I like action movies. Do you?

B: No, but I like animated movies. Do you?

Lesson B `Do you remember?`
Match the questions with the suggestions. You have one minute.

1 We should see a movie. Do you have any suggestions? _____
2 I'm hungry. Any suggestions? _____
3 Let's get some exercise. What do you suggest? _____
4 Where should we go shopping? Any suggestions? _____
5 We need to take a vacation? What do you suggest? _____

a We could take a walk.
b Why don't we go to the market?
c We could see a comedy.
d Why don't we go to Mexico?
e Let's make pizza!

Lesson C `Brainstorm!`
Make a list of types of music. How many do you know? Take turns. You and your partner have two minutes.

Lesson D `Guess!`
Describe a popular band or singer, but don't say the name. Can your partner guess the name? Take turns. You and your partner have two minutes.

A: She sings pop music. She sings in Korean and Japanese. She's also an actress.

B: BoA?

A: Yes. Her real name is Kwon Bo-ah.

2 In the real world

What were some of the top movies this year? Go online and find information about one of them in English. Then write about it.

- What's the name of the movie?
- What actors are in it?
- What type of movie is it?
- What songs are in the movie?

A Top Movie

. . . was one of the top movies this year.
It's an animated movie . . .

12 Time for a change

Warm-up

A The people in the pictures have made changes in their lives. What change do you think each person made?

B Would you like to make any of these changes? Which ones?

A Personal change

1 Vocabulary Personal goals

A 🎧 Match the words and the pictures. Then listen and check your answers.

a	get a credit card	**d**	lose weight	**g**	save money
b	join a gym	**e**	make more friends	**h**	start a new hobby
c	learn an instrument	**f**	pass a test	**i**	work / study harder

 1 ☐

 2 ☐

 3 ☐

 4 ☐

 5 ☐

 6 ☐

 7 ☐

 8 ☐

 9 ☐

B **PAIR WORK** Which things in Part A are easy to do? Which are more difficult? Why? Tell your partner.

"It's difficult to learn an instrument. It takes a long time!"

2 Language in context I'm making it happen!

A 🎧 Listen to three people talk about changes. Who's learning something new?

My friends and I are starting our own band next year. I can sing, but I can't play an instrument, so I'm taking a class to learn the guitar.

–Leonardo

I joined a gym last month to lose weight. I only want to lose a couple of kilos, but I'm finding it difficult. But I'm making some new friends, so that's good.

–Mark

I hated taking the bus to work, so I saved money to buy a bike. Now I ride it to work every day, and I feel a lot healthier and happier.

–Tina

B Talk about a change you made.

3 Grammar 🎧 Infinitives of purpose

I'm taking a class **to learn** the guitar.	(= because I want to learn the guitar)
I joined a gym last month **to lose** weight.	(= because I want to lose weight)
She'd like to save money **to buy** a bike.	(= because she wants to buy a bike)
We're starting a book club in July **to make** more friends.	(= because we want to make more friends)

A Match the sentence parts. Then compare with a partner.

1 I joined a gym last week   to buy a car.

2 I'm saving my money   to get better grades.

3 I'd like to go to the U.S.   to relax.

4 I studied harder   to improve my English.

5 I listen to music   to lose weight.

B Rewrite these sentences. Use an infinitive of purpose. Then compare with a partner.

1 I'd like to go to a hair salon because I want to get a new hairstyle.

    I'd like to go to a hair salon to get a new hairstyle.

2 I listen to songs in English because I want to improve my listening.

    _____

3 I saved my money because I wanted to buy a new computer.

    _____

4 I'm studying on weekends because I want to get a better job.

    _____

C **PAIR WORK** Which sentences from Part B are true for you? Tell your partner.

4 Speaking Three changes

A Complete the chart with three changes you would like to make. Then think about the reasons why you would like to make each change.

	Changes	Reasons
1		
2		
3		

B **GROUP WORK** Discuss your changes. Are any of your changes or reasons the same?

"I'd like to go to Canada to study English. I hope to be an English teacher someday."

5 Keep talking!

Go to page 151 for more practice.

I can give reasons for personal changes. ✓

B I'm happy to hear that!

1 Interactions Good and bad news

A Do you ever see old classmates or friends around town? What kinds of things do you talk about?

B 🎧 Listen to the conversation. What's changed for Emily? Then practice the conversation.

Joe	Hey, Emily. Long time no see.
Emily	Oh, hi, Joe. How are you doing?
Joe	Fine. Well, actually, I didn't pass my driving test – again. That's three times now.
Emily	That's too bad.
Joe	Yeah, I wanted to drive to the beach this weekend. So, what's new with you?

Emily	Well, I'm playing guitar in a band. I'm really enjoying it.
Joe	That's wonderful! What kind of music?
Emily	Rock. We have a show next week. Do you want to come? I'll email you the information.
Joe	Thanks. I'll be there!

C 🎧 Listen to the expressions. Then practice the conversation again with the new expressions.

Reacting to bad news

That's too bad.   That's a shame.   I'm sorry to hear that.

Reacting to good news

That's wonderful!   That's great to hear!   I'm happy to hear that!

D **PAIR WORK** Share the news below and react appropriately.

I'm learning German.	I lost my wallet.
I bought a car.	I won two concert tickets.
I failed my math exam.	I'm going to travel to London.
I have a part-time job.	I'm not sleeping well.
I broke my foot.	I'm planning to get a pet.

2 Listening Sharing news

A Look at the pictures in Part B. Where are the people?

B 🎧 Listen to four people share news with friends. What news are they talking about? Number the pictures from 1 to 4.

C 🎧 Listen again. Correct the false sentences. Then compare with a partner.

1 Mark has some free time in the afternoons and evenings.

2 Lucia is saving her money to buy a restaurant.

3 Jeff is taking the train because his new car isn't running very well.

4 Wendy and her cousin had a terrible time in Rome and Florence.

3 Speaking Good news, bad news

A Complete the chart with some good news and bad news. (Don't use true news!)

	Good news		Bad news
1		1	
2		2	

B Class activity Share your news. React appropriately.

A: Hi, Mariko. What's new with you?

B: Well, I'm going to Paris next week to study French.

A: That's wonderful!

B: What's new with you?

C GROUP WORK Share the most interesting news you heard.

I can react to good and bad news. ✓

C I think I'll get a job.

1 Vocabulary Milestones

A 🎧 Complete the chart with the correct milestones. Then listen and check your answers.

☐ buy a house   ☐ get promoted   ☐ go to college

☐ graduate from high school   ☐ rent an apartment   ☐ retire

☐ start a career   ☐ get married   ☐ start school

Personal milestones	Educational milestones	Work-related milestones

B Number the milestones from 1 to 9 in the order that they usually happen. Then compare with a partner.

2 Conversation I'll go traveling.

A 🎧 Listen and practice.

Tim Hey, Craig. How are you doing?

Craig Oh, hi, Tim. I'm fine. What's new with you?

Tim Well, I'm graduating from college this summer.

Craig That's wonderful! What do you think you'll do in September?

Tim I think I'll go traveling with some friends.

Craig That sounds fun, but it won't be cheap.

Tim Yeah, so I may get a job this summer to pay for the trip.

B 🎧 Listen to the rest of the conversation. What's new with Craig?

3 Grammar 🎧 *Will* for predictions; *may*, *might* for possibility

What do you think you'll do?	
Predictions I think **I'll go** traveling with some friends. I **won't get** a roommate. Do you think you**'ll get** a roommate? Yes, I**'ll get** one soon. No. I **won't get** a roommate this year.	*Possibility* I don't really know. I **may get** a job. I'm not really sure. I **might buy** a pet.

A Circle the correct words. Then practice with a partner.

1 A Do you think you'll buy a house next year?

   B No. I don't have enough money. But **I'll / I may** rent an apartment. I don't know.

2 A What do you think you'll do on your next birthday?

   B **I'll / I might** have a big party, but I'm not sure.

3 A When do you think you'll retire?

   B **I'll / I may** retire at 65. Most other people do.

4 A Do you think you'll buy a car this year?

   B No, **I won't / I might**. I don't have enough money for one.

5 A Do you think you'll get married after college?

   B I'm not sure. **I'll / I may** get married someday.

B PAIR WORK Ask and answer the questions in Part A. Answer with your own information.

4 Pronunciation Contraction of *will*

🎧 Listen and repeat. Notice how these pronouns + *will* are contracted into one syllable.

I'll   you'll   he'll   she'll   we'll   they'll

5 Speaking My future

A Write an idea for each of the things below.

1 an important thing to do: _____

2 an exciting thing to do: _____

3 an expensive thing to buy: _____

4 an interesting person to meet: _____

B PAIR WORK Ask and answer questions about the things in Part A. Use *will*, *may*, or *might* and these time expressions.

A: *Do you think you'll start your career this year?*

B: *Yes, I think I will. I have an interview this week.*

Time expressions	
this week	this month
this weekend	next month
next week	this year

6 Keep talking!

Go to page 152 for more practice.

I can make predictions about the future. ✓

D Dreams and aspirations

1 Reading 🎧

A Look at this quote. What do you think it means?

"The important thing in life is not to win but to try."

–Pierre de Coubertin, founder of the modern Olympic games

B Read the article. Check (✓) the best title.

☐ Skater Loses Olympics but Wins Fans

☐ An Olympic Dream Flies High

☐ The Worst Olympian Ever

☐ Ski Jumper – or Ski Dropper?

At the 1988 Winter Olympics, the most famous competitor wasn't the fastest skier or the strongest ice skater. He didn't win a gold medal – or any medals at all. In fact, Eddie Edwards finished last in the ski jumping competition. But his courage made him a favorite of fans around the world, who nicknamed him "Eddie the Eagle."

Eddie was a construction worker from a small town in England. He had a dream to make the Olympic team.

He was a good skier and almost made the British team in 1984. For the 1988 games, he became England's #1 ski jumper for a simple reason – nobody else wanted to try.

Eddie had no money and no coach. He saved money to buy used equipment – his ski boots were too big, so he wore six pairs of socks. He didn't see very well and wore thick glasses. "Sometimes I take off, and I can't see where I'm going," he said. Before each jump, he was afraid that he might fall. But he worked hard to learn and to improve.

At the Olympic Games in Calgary, Eddie competed in the 70m and 90m jumps. He landed without falling, but came in last in both events.

Many people loved Eddie for his dream and his courage. But others thought he wasn't good enough to compete. To these people, Eddie said, "Where is it written that the Olympics are only for winners?"

Eddie's performance made him famous in England. When he returned home, 10,000 people met him at the airport. Today, Eddie is a construction worker again, but he is also famous thanks to the 2016 film, "Eddie the Eagle."

C Read the article again. Answer the questions.

1 What was Eddie's dream? _____

2 What was Eddie afraid of? _____

3 Why did the crowd like Eddie? _____

4 Why did many people like Eddie? _____

D GROUP WORK Do you think it's more important to win or to try? Should the Olympic Games be open to athletes like Eddie, or only the best athletes?

2 Listening An interview with an athlete

A 🎧 **Listen to an interview with Suzanne, a marathon runner. Check (✓) the two dreams she's achieved.**

☐ to run marathons
☐ to go back to school
☐ to win the Chicago Marathon
☐ to run all the big marathons

B 🎧 **Listen again. Circle the correct answers.**

1 This is Suzanne's **fifth** / **seventh** marathon.

2 She **won** / **didn't win** the Boston Marathon.

3 She finished **first** / **last** in her first race in high school.

4 At age **39** / **43**, she decided to make some changes in her life.

5 The most difficult thing for her was the **training** / **stress**.

3 Writing A dream come true

A **Think of a dream that came true for you. Answer the questions.**

● What was your dream?   ● Why was it a dream for you?   ● How did your dream come true?

B **Write about your dream. Use the model and your answers in Part A to help you.**

> **My Dream**
> My dream was to study Mexican cooking in Oaxaca. I loved to cook, but
> I wasn't a very good cook. So I went to Oaxaca to study Mexican cooking.
> I took a two-week class. It was a dream come true. Now I can make
> great meals. Who knows? I might become a chef someday.

C GROUP WORK **Share your writing. Ask and answer questions for more information.**

4 Speaking Dream planner

A **Complete the chart with a dream for the future. Then add three things you'll need to do to achieve it.**

My Dream	How I'll make it happen
	1
	2
	3

B GROUP WORK **Tell your group about your dream and how you'll achieve it.**

A: My dream is to start my own business someday.

B: That's a great dream. How will you make it happen?

A: Well, first I'll go back to school. Then I'll get a job to get some experience.

I can discuss my dreams for the future. ✓

Wrap-up

1 Quick pair review

Lesson A [Brainstorm!]
Make a list of personal goals that people can have. How many do you know? You have two minutes.

Lesson B [Do you remember?]
Write B for ways to react to bad news. Write G for ways to react to good news. You have one minute.

1 _____ That's too bad.

2 _____ I'm sorry to hear that.

3 _____ That's wonderful!

4 _____ I'm happy to hear that!

5 _____ That's a shame.

6 _____ That's great to hear!

Lesson C [Find out!]
What are two things both you and your partner think you will do in the future? Take turns. You and your partner have two minutes.

A: I think I'll go to college in two years.

B: I don't think I will. I may travel first.

Lesson D [Guess!]
Describe a dream you had when you were a child. Can your partner guess what it was? Take turns. You and your partner have two minutes.

A: I loved swimming. I wanted to win a gold medal.

B: Did you want to swim in the Olympics?

A: Yes, I did.

2 In the real world

What future goals do famous people have? Do you think they will achieve them? Go online and find information in English about a famous person in one of these categories. Then write about him or her.

| an actor | an athlete | a businessperson | a politician | a scientist | a singer |

Bill Gates
Bill Gates wants to improve people's health.
I think he'll achieve this goal . . .

Which product is . . .?

A **PAIR WORK** Add two more products to the chart. Then think of two examples you know for each product and write their names in the chart.

	Example 1	Example 2	
Video game			Which is newer? Which is more fun? Which is . . .?
Computer			Which is easier to use? Which is faster? Which is . . .?
Cell phone			Which is thinner? Which is less expensive? Which is . . .?
Car			Which is smaller? Which is faster? Which is . . .?

B Compare each pair of products. Use the questions in Part A and your own ideas.

  A: I think . . . is newer than . . .

  B: That's right. It's more fun, too.

  A: I don't really agree. I think . . . is more fun. My friends and I can play it all day!

C Share your comparisons with the class. Which product is better? Why?

They aren't big enough!

Student A

You and your partner have pictures of the same people, but there are eight differences. Describe the pictures and ask questions about the differences. Circle them.

A: In my picture, Nancy's pants are too baggy. They look very uncomfortable.

B: In my picture, Nancy's pants are too tight. So, that's different.

A: What about Maria's pants? I think they're too short.

B: They're too short in my picture, too. So, that's the same.

Keep talking!

From the past

Student A

A PAIR WORK You and your partner have information on six famous people from the past, but some information is missing. Ask these questions and complete the information.

- Where was . . . born?
- What did . . . do?
- When was . . . born?
- Why was . . . famous?

Name	George Washington	Frida Kahlo	Charlie Chaplin
Place of birth	the U.S.	Mexico	England
Date of birth	February 22, 1732	July 6, 1907	_____
What did	_____	painter	actor and director
Why famous	He was the first president of the U.S.	She was very _____, and her art was _____.	He was in a lot of funny black-and-white movies.

 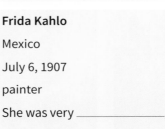 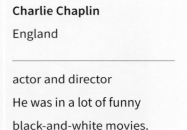

Name	Jesse Owens	Marie Curie	Yuri Gagarin
Place of birth	the U.S.	_____	Russia
Date of birth	September 12, 1913	November 7, 1867	March 9, 1934
What did	athlete	scientist	astronaut
Why famous	He was the first American to win _____ gold _____ in track and field in one Olympics.	She was the first person to win two Nobel prizes.	He was the first person in _____.

B PAIR WORK Look at the information. What similarities can you find between these famous people and other famous people you know?

What can you do here?

A PAIR WORK Think about where you live. Where can you do each of these things? Take notes.

hear live music

see interesting dance

buy fun souvenirs

eat good, cheap food

see statues and art

enjoy beautiful views

go for a walk

visit historical sites

enjoy nature

A: You can often hear live music at the city square.

B: Right. And there's also the university coffee shop.

A: That's true. They have live music on Fridays and Saturdays.

B GROUP WORK Share your information. How similar are your ideas?

Keep talking!

City quiz

A PAIR WORK Take the quiz. Ask the questions and guess the answers. Take turns.

1 What is the biggest city in North America?
   a Mexico City   b Los Angeles   c Washington, D.C.

2 Where is the biggest soccer stadium in South America?
   a Buenos Aires, Argentina b Rio de Janeiro, Brazil c Lima, Peru

3 "The Big Apple" is the nickname for what U.S. city?
   a Boston   b Washington, D.C.   c New York City

4 Which city is on the Han River?
   a New Orleans, U.S.   b Venice, Italy   c Seoul, South Korea

5 What is the most expensive city?
   a Tokyo, Japan   b London, England   c Rome, Italy

6 What is the safest big city in the U.S.?
   a New York City   b Las Vegas   c Boston

7 The oldest subway system in the world is in what European city?
   a Paris, France   b Madrid, Spain   c London, England

8 Which city has the worst traffic in the U.S.?
   a Chicago   b Los Angeles   c San Francisco

9 What city is in both Europe and Asia?
   a Berlin, Germany   b Stockholm, Sweden   c Istanbul, Turkey

10 The biggest public square in the world is in what city?
   a Beijing, China   b Moscow, Russia   c London, England

B Check your answers on the bottom of this page. How many did you get correct?

C PAIR WORK Think of another question and three possible answer choices. Ask another pair.
Do they know the answer?

"What's the largest city in . . .?"

1.a   2.b   3.c   4.c   5.a   6.a   7.c   8.b   9.c   10.a

Keep talking!

143

They aren't big enough!

Student B

You and your partner have pictures of the same people, but there are eight differences. Describe the pictures and ask questions about the differences. Circle them.

A: In my picture, Nancy's pants are too baggy. They look very uncomfortable.

B: In my picture, Nancy's pants are too tight. So, that's different.

A: What about Maria's pants? I think they're too short.

B: They're too short in my picture, too. So, that's the same.

Keep talking!

From the Past

Student B

A PAIR WORK You and your partner have information about six famous people from the past, but some information is missing. Ask these questions and complete the information.

- Where was . . . born?
- When was . . . born?
- What did . . . do?
- Why was . . . famous?

Name	George Washington	Frida Kahlo	Charlie Chaplin
Place of birth	the U.S.	_____	England
Date of birth	February 22, 1732	July 6, 1907	April 16, 1889
What did	politician	painter	actor and director
Why famous	He was the first _____ of the _____.	She was very creative, and her art was very interesting.	He was in a lot of _____ black-and-white _____.

Name	Jesse Owens	Marie Curie	Yuri Gagarin
Place of birth	the U.S.	Poland	Russia
Date of birth	_____	November 7, 1867	March 9, 1934
What did	athlete	scientist	_____
Why famous	He was the first American to win four gold medals in track and field in one Olympics.	She was the first person to win _____ Nobel _____.	He was the first person in space.

B PAIR WORK Look at the information. What similarities can you find between these famous people and other famous people you know?

What an inspiring person!

A Think of three people you admire. Use the categories below or think of your own. Then complete the chart.

an athlete   a musician   a writer   an artist   a scientist
a politician an actor/actress a business leader a family member a teacher

	Name	Why	Notes
1			
2			
3			

B GROUP WORK Share your ideas. Ask and answer questions for more information.

A: I really admire Sergey Brin and Larry Page. They started Google.

B: Why do you admire them?

A: Well, I think they're both talented and intelligent.

C: Do you think they're also . . .?

C Is there a famous person who you *don't* admire? Why not?

Keep talking!

A one-of-a-kind menu

A GROUP WORK Imagine you're going to open a restaurant together. Answer the questions and create a menu.

- What's the name of your restaurant?
- What do you want to serve?
- Is it a cheap or an expensive restaurant? Write the prices.

_____ Restaurant

APPETIZERS

MAIN DISHES

SIDE DISHES

DESSERTS

DRINKS

A: Let's have three or four appetizers.

B: OK. How about some garlic bread and onion soup?

C: That sounds good. Let's have a salad, too. How about . . .?

B GROUP WORK Exchange your menus. Ask and answer questions about the items. Which dishes would you order?

A: The Mexican salad sounds interesting. What's in it?

B: It has lettuce, tomatoes, onions, peppers, beans, and corn.

Yes, I have.

GROUP WORK **Play the game. Put a small object on** *Start*. **Toss a coin.**

 Move 1 space.

Heads

 Move 2 spaces.

Tails

Use the words to ask and answer questions. Ask your own *Have you ever . . . ?* questions on the **Free question** spaces. Take turns.

A: Have you ever made French fries?

B: Yes, I have.

Keep talking!

Movie favorites

A Complete the chart with six types of movies that you like. Add a title for each type.

	Type of movie	Title of movie
1		
2		
3		
4		
5		
6		

B **CLASS ACTIVITY** Find classmates who like the same types of movies you like. Then ask questions with *Have you ever . . . ?*

A: I really like animated movies.

B: So do I.

A: Really? Have you ever seen *Despicable Me?*

B: Yes, I have. I love that movie!

Class Survey

A Complete the questions with your own ideas.

1 Do you like the band _____?
     (a band) ☐

2 Do you like the song _____?
     (a song title) ☐

3 Do you have the album _____?
     (name of an album) ☐

4 Do you ever listen to _____?
     (a type of music) ☐

5 Do you know the words to the song _____?
     (name of a song) ☐

6 Did you listen to _____ as a child?
     (a type of music) ☐

7 Would you like to see _____ in concert?
     (a singer or band) ☐

B CLASS ACTIVITY Ask your classmates the questions in Part A. How many people said "yes" to each question? Write the total number in the boxes.

C PAIR WORK Share your information.

A: A lot of our classmates like the band . . .

B: That's interesting. Not many of us like the band . . .

D Share the most interesting information with the class.

"All of us would like to see . . . in concert."

Keep talking!

Why did I do that?

A Think about things that you did in the past. Check (✓) the things in the first column that are true for you. Then add three more things.

☐ I took a long trip   to _____ .

☐ I sent a text to someone   to _____ .

☐ I took a test   to _____ .

☐ I joined a gym   to _____ .

☐ I got a cell phone   to _____ .

☐ I uploaded some photos   to _____ .

☐ I worked hard   to _____ .

☐ I got a part time job   to _____ .

☐ _____   to _____ .

☐ _____   to _____ .

☐ _____   to _____ .

B Why did you do each thing? Complete the sentences in Part A with an infinitive of purpose. Use the ideas below or think of your own.

talk with my friends	learn an instrument	show my friends
get my driver's license	get some experience	get a job
share good news	buy a gift	make more friends
save money	lose weight	see my relatives

C **GROUP WORK** Share your sentences. Ask and answer questions for more information.

A: I took a long trip to see my relatives.

B: When was that?

A: Last year.

C: Where did you go?

A: I went . . .

Next year . . .

A Add two future activities to the chart.

Do you think you'll . . . next year?	Name	Other details
take a trip with your family		
start a new hobby		
join a gym		
get married		
buy something expensive		
move to a different home		
start a career		
learn a musical instrument		

B CLASS ACTIVITY Find classmates who will do each thing. Write their names. Ask and answer questions for more information. Take notes.

A: Jun, *do you think you'll take a trip with your family next year?*

B: Yes, I do.

A: Really? Where will you go?

B: We're planning to go to Australia to visit some friends. I hope to . . .

C GROUP WORK Share the most interesting information.

Keep talking!

Irregular verbs

Base form	Simple past	Past Participle
be	was, were	been
become	became	become
build	built	built
buy	bought	bought
choose	chose	chosen
come	came	come
do	did	done
draw	drew	drawn
drink	drank	drunk
drive	drove	driven
eat	ate	eaten
feel	felt	felt
get	got	gotten
give	gave	given
go	went	gone
hang	hung	hung
have	had	had
hear	heard	heard
hold	held	held
know	knew	known
leave	left	left
lose	lost	lost
make	made	made

Base form	Simple past	Past Participle
meet	met	met
pay	paid	paid
put	put	put
read	read	read
ride	rode	ridden
run	ran	run
say	said	said
see	saw	seen
sell	sold	sold
send	sent	sent
sing	sang	sung
sit	sat	sat
sleep	slept	slept
speak	spoke	spoken
spend	spent	spent
stand	stood	stood
swim	swam	swum
take	took	taken
teach	taught	taught
think	thought	thought
wear	wore	worn
win	won	won
write	wrote	written

Credits

The authors and publishers acknowledge the following sources of copyright material and are grateful for the permissions granted. While every effort has been made, it has not always been possible to identify the sources of all the material used, or to trace all copyright holders. If any omissions are brought to our notice, we will be happy to include the appropriate acknowledgements on reprinting and in the next update to the digital edition, as applicable.

Photography
All below images are sourced from Getty Images.
Front Matter: Hero Images; **U1:** Rob Ball/WireImage; Chris J Ratcliffe/Stringer/Getty Images News; Bulat Silvia/iStock/Getty Images Plus; Rick Doyle/The Image Bank; Maxiphoto/iStock/Getty Images Plus; pashapixel/iStock/Getty Images Plus; empire331/iStock/Getty Images Plus; Shuji Kobayashi/The Image Bank; tioloco/iStock/Getty Images Plus; artisteer/iStock/Getty Images Plus; onurdongel/E+; Digital Vision; KidStock/Blend Images; 4x6/iStock/Getty Images Plus; Kris Timken/Blend Images; Patrik Giardino/Corbis; BakiBG/E+; Donald Miralle/DigitalVision; Robert Daly/OJO Images; Gary Burchell/DigitalVision; Westend61/Brand X Pictures; EXTREME-PHOTOGRAPHER/E+; Thinkstock/Stockbyte; digitalfarmer/iStock/Getty Images Plus; Westend61; JGI/Jamie Grill/Blend Images; Hannah Foslien/Getty Images Sport; **U2:** Alexander Spatari/Moment; Mark Edward Atkinson/Tracey Lee/Blend Images; milehightraveler/E+; damircudic/E+; JGI/Jamie Grill/Blend Images; Blue Images/Corbis; Wavebreakmedia/iStock/Getty Images Plus; Asia Images Group; KaVaStudio2015/iStock/Getty Images Plus; PeopleImages/E+; Purestock; Tanya Constantine/Blend Images; alvarez/E+; Firda Beka; Ronnie Kaufman/Larry Hirshowitz/Blend Images; Image Source; Dominique Charriau/WireImage; **U3:** Andersen Ross/DigitalVision; Matthew Lloyd/Stringer/Getty Images News; SeanPavonePhoto/iStock Editorial/Getty Images Plus; SteffenWalter/iStock Editorial/Getty Images Plus; gpointstudio/iStock/Getty Images Plus; Mats Silvan/Moment; technotr/Vetta; VV-pics/iStock/Getty Images Plus; icholakov/iStock/Getty Images Plus; JodiJacobson/E+; Glowimages; Georgia Immins/EyeEm; Getty Images; Alex Robinson/robertharding; Robert Francis/robertharding; Fouque/iStock/Getty Images Plus; Andrew Lichtenstein/Corbis News; sebastianosecondi/iStock/Getty Images Plus; Shannon Fagan; pavlen/iStock/Getty Images Plus; RichLegg/iStock/Getty Images Plus; Peter Dennen; Chris Speedie; Raimund Linke; hudiemm/iStock/Getty Images Plus; Denyshutter/iStock/Getty Images Plus; PhotoObjects.net/Getty Images Plus; Comstock/Stockbyte; TopPhotoImages/iStock/Getty Images Plus; Chen Liu/EyeEm; **U4:** Jumping Rocks; arnitorfason/iStock/Getty Images Plus; dabldy/iStock Editorial/Getty Images Plus; Aleksandr_Kendenkov/iStock/Getty Images Plus; JazzIRT/E+; Chefmd/iStock/Getty Images Plus; ennesseePhotographer/iStock Editorial/Getty Images Plus; Gunter Marx Photography/Corbis Documentary; Tatjana Kaufmann; Laurie Noble/Stone; Bettmann; Jon Hicks/The Image Bank; NurPhoto; WolfeLarry/iStock/Getty Images Plus; John Rensten/The Image Bank; Siri Stafford/DigitalVision; hulya-erkisi/iStock/Getty Images Plus; Eerik/iStock/Getty Images Plus; fStop Images - Patrick Strattner/Brand X Pictures; TommL/iStock/Getty Images Plus; Eco Images/Universal Images Group; shironosov/iStock/Getty Images Plus; **U5:** Jupiterimages/Pixland/Getty Images Plus; Matthieu Spohn/PhotoAlto Agency RF Collections; Niedring/Drentwett/MITO images; RichVintage/E+; Purestock; Westend61; Peathegee Inc/Blend Images; Hola Images; YKD/iStock/Getty Images Plus; kellll/iStock/Getty Images Plus; energyy/iStock/Getty Images Plus; drbimages/E+; zegers06/iStock/Getty Images Plus; Peter Dazeley/Photographer's Choice; dima_sidelnikov/iStock/Getty Images Plus; laindiapiaroa/Blend Images/Getty Images Plus; Highwaystarz-Photography/iStock/Getty Images Plus; Eva-Katalin/E+; bagotaj/iStock/Getty Images Plus; Clerkenwell/Vetta; Tom Merton/OJO Images; South_agency/iStock/Getty Images Plus; B. Boissonnet; paylessimages/iStock/Getty Images Plus; hxdbzxy/iStock/Getty Images Plus; Image Source/Photodisc; Jose Luis Pelaez Inc/Blend Images; Dougal Waters/DigitalVision; Brand X; Alen-D/iStock/Getty Images Plus; Hero Images; shironosov/iStock/Getty Images Plus; Robert van 't Hoenderdaal/iStock Editorial/Getty Images Plus; Simon McGill/Moment; nensuria/iStock/Getty Images Plus; Peter Dazeley/Photographer's Choice; Velvetfish/iStock/Getty Images Plus; undefined/iStock/Getty Images Plus; onepony/iStock/Getty Images Plus; Olga_k_/iStock/Getty Images Plus; studiocasper/iStock/Getty Images Plus; Pascal Broze/ONOKY; **U6:** Fernando Trabanco Fotografía/Moment; Tara Moore/Corbis; Jacob Wackerhausen/iStock/Getty Images Plus; Chris Ryan/Caiaimage; BJI/Blue Jean Images; Alija/Vetta; Lorado/E+; DreamPictures/Stone; Chud/Moment; Andy Rouse/The Image Bank; Erik Dreyer/Stone; powerofforever/E+; simonkr/E+; Vicki Jauron, Babylon and Beyond/Moment; Klaus Vedfelt/DigitalVision; Charley Gallay/Getty Images Entertainment; hikesterson/iStock/Getty Images Plus; RUNSTUDIO/DigitalVision; Matt Jelonek/WireImage; **U7:** Kathrin Ziegler/Taxi; Mike Watson Images/moodboard/Getty Images Plus; gradyreese/E+; Thomas Barwick/Photodisc; John S Lander/LightRocket; gracethang/iStock Editorial/Getty Images Plus; Jeff Greenberg/Universal Images Group; anyaberkut/iStock/Getty Images Plus; Nerthuz/iStock/Getty Images Plus; Dieter Spears/EyeEm; 3dgoksu/iStock/Getty Images Plus; 3drenderings/iStock/Getty Images Plus; Marco Rosario Venturini Autieri/iStock/Getty Images Plus; luismmolina/iStock/Getty Images Plus; ZargonDesign/E+; Chris Collins/Corbis; mladn61/iStock/Getty Images Plus; PC Plus Magazine/Future; cleotis/iStock/Getty Images Plus; pongky.n/iStock/Getty Images Plus; nevodka/iStock/Getty Images Plus; ItsraSanprasert/iStock/Getty Images Plus; MarkELaw/iStock/Getty Images Plus; Paolo_Toffanin/iStock/Getty Images Plus; digitalskillet/iStock/Getty Images Plus; naumoid/iStock/Getty Images Plus; richjem/iStock/Getty Images Plus; rasslava/iStock/Getty Images Plus; arogant/iStock/Getty Images Plus; momcilog/iStock/Getty Images Plus; emreogan/iStock/Getty Images Plus; lypnyk2/iStock/Getty Images Plus; Wulf Voss/EyeEm; Tarzhanova/iStock/Getty Images Plus; panic_attack/iStock/Getty Images Plus; Feng Li/Staff/Getty Images Entertainment; Chen Chao; Maremagnum/Photolibrary; Martin_Szczepaniak/iStock Editorial/Getty Images Plus; DC_Colombia/iStock Editorial/Getty Images Plus; **U8:** guruXOOX/iStock/Getty Images Plus; Pawel.gaul/E+; Kevin Forest/Photodisc; studyoritim/iStock/Getty Images Plus; Grant Faint/The Image Bank; Richard Baker/In Pictures; TOLGA AKMEN/AFP; Westend61; FotoDuets/iStock Editorial/Getty Images Plus; csfotoimages/iStock Editorial/Getty Images Plus; Luis Dafos/Moment; imantsu/iStock/Getty Images Plus; rachel/iStock/Getty Images Plus; Martin Wahlborg/iStock/Getty Images Plus; Ed-Ni-Photo/iStock Editorial/Getty Images Plus; Richard T. Nowitz/Corbis Documentary; bluejayphoto/iStock Editorial/Getty Images Plus; VitalyEdush/iStock/Getty Images Plus; baona/iStock/Getty Images Plus; MAURO PIMENTEL/AFP; holgs/iStock/Getty Images Plus; shomos uddin/Moment; Dmitry Ageev/Blend Images; Cavan Images/Cavan; BRANDONJ74/E+; Carlos Ciudad Photos/Moment; Maskot; Wei Fang/Moment; **U9:** Michael Gottschalk/Photothek; Pablo Cuadra/Getty Images Entertainment; Stock Montage/Archive Photos; Mehdi Taamallah/NurPhoto; Kelvin Ma/Bloomberg; Jason LaVeris/FilmMagic; RG-vc/iStock/Getty Images Plus; kickers/iStock/Getty Images Plus; bjones27/E+; Reuben Krabbe/Ascent Xmedia/Photodisc; Jupiterimages/Goodshoot/Getty Images Plus; STR/AFP; DreamPictures/Blend Images; skynesher/E+; Comstock Images/Stockbyte; VANDERLEI ALMEIDA/AFP; ben radford/Corbis Sport; Apic/Hulton Archive; Library of Congress/Corbis Historical/VCG; David Levenson/Getty Images Entertainment; JOSE CENDON/AFP; Bettmann; Mahmoud Khaled/Anadolu Agency; THOMAS COEX/AFP; Chris Ratcliffe/Bloomberg; Wavebreakmedia; **U10:** Blulz60/iStock Editorial/Getty Images Plus; john shepherd/iStock/Getty Images Plus; Anastassios Mentis/Stockbyte; kajakiki/E+; Inna Zakharchenko/iStock/Getty Images Plus; WolfeLarry/iStock/Getty Images Plus; Sunwoo Jung/DigitalVision; Vostok/Moment; Jon Hicks/Corbis Documentary; effrey Greenberg/Universal Images Group; Photodisc; bhofack2/iStock/Getty Images Plus; rebeccafondren/iStock/Getty Images Plus; Asia Images Group; HariKarki2003/iStock/Getty Images Plus; naruedom/iStock/Getty Images Plus; mikdam/iStock/Getty Images Plus; NightAndDayImages/E+; margouillatphotos/iStock/Getty Images Plus; Amarita/iStock/Getty Images Plus; 3dsguru/iStock/Getty Images Plus; Boogich/iStock/Getty Images Plus; EmirMemedovski/E+; whitewish/iStock/Getty Images Plus; India Today Group; PeopleImages/E+; Eurngkwan/iStock/Getty Images Plus; **U11:** Hero Images; Emmanuel Faure/The Image Bank; Joe McBride/The Image Bank; izusek/iStock/Getty Images Plus; Hugh Sitton/Stone; John Lamb/The Image Bank; Denkou Images/Cultura; Chud/Moment; Westend61; Hill Street Studios/Blend Images; Michael Klippfeld/Moment; mmac72/E+; Stephanie Rausser/DigitalVision; andresr/E+; Crazytang/E+; Anadolu Agency/Anadolu Agency; Ryan Smith/Corbis; olmozott98/iStock Editorial/Getty Images Plus; Rubberball/Mike Kemp; Onradio/iStock/Getty Images Plus; JGI/Tom Grill/Blend Images; Mlenny/iStock/Getty Images Plus; Inti St. Clair/DigitalVision; Bokeshi/iStock/Getty Images Plus; DreamPictures/Blend Images; Alexei Cruglicov/iStock/Getty Images Plus; piovesempre/iStock/Getty Images Plus; Michael Luhrenberg/iStock/Getty Images Plus; JGI/Tom Grill/Blend Images; Jose Luis Pelaez Inc/Blend Images; moodboard/Cultura; Gabriel Rossi/LatinContent WO; Nilanka Sampath/iStock/Getty Images Plus; Vera_Petrunina/iStock/Getty Images Plus; John Parra; BaloOm Studios/Moment; **U12:** Kemter/iStock/Getty Images Plus; Jetta Productions Inc/DigitalVision; PJPhoto69/iStock/Getty Images Plus; Westend61; Caia Image/Mix: Subjects; Studio CJ/E+; shank_ali/E+; Dougal Waters/DigitalVision; john shepherd/iStock/Getty Images Plus; Neustockimages/E+; laughingmango/iStock/Getty Images Plus; Eakachai Leesin/EyeEm; Jose Luis Pelaez Inc/Blend Images; JGI/Tom Grill/Blend Images; Tomas Rodriguez/Corbis stockyimages/iStock/Getty Images Plus; Michael H/DigitalVision; Thinkstock Images/Stockbyte; Blend Images; Design Pics; Paul Bradbury/OJO Images; Predrag Vuckovic/E+; Moma7/iStock/Getty Images Plus; aldomurillo/E+; fstop123/iStock/Getty Images Plus; Blend Images - JGI/Jamie Grill/Brand X Pictures; Erstudiostok/iStock/Getty Images Plus; tommaso79/ iStock/Getty Images Plus; David Cannon/Allsport; John Lamparski/Getty Images Entertainment; **End Matter:** golovorez/iStock/Getty Images Plus; afe207/iStock/Getty Images Plus; ugurv/iStock/Getty Images Plus; Doug Byrnes/Corbis; GoodLifeStudio/iStock/Getty Images Plus; Mongkhon bualaphum/iStock/Getty Images Plus; C Squared Studios/Photodisc; Raquel Pedrosa/Moment Open; Fandrade/Moment Open; PeopleImages/iStock/Getty Images Plus; John Greim/LightRocket; Alex Robinson Photography/Moment; Wavebreak/iStock/Getty Images Plus; Westend61; SolStock/E+; Icon Sportswire; Kenny McCartney/Moment; JGI/Jamie Grill/Blend Images; Geber86/E+; Purestock; YinYang/E+; skynesher/E+; Maskot; Squaredpixels/E+; Caiaimage/Paul Bradbury; Image Source/DigitalVision; PhonlamaiPhoto/iStock/Getty Images Plus; fazon1/iStock/Getty Images Plus; zhudifeng/iStock/Getty Images Plus; miflippo/iStock/Getty Images Plus; Dougal Waters/Photographer's Choice; Juanmonino/iStock/Getty Images Plus; Ron Levine/Stockbyte; Fuse/Corbis; Jon Feingersh/Blend Images; Igor Emmerich/Corbis/VCG/Corbis; Saro17/E+; Brand X Pictures/Stokebyte; Sergey Nazarov/iStock/Getty Images Plus; Gwengoat/iStock/Getty Images Plus; Hulton Archive; Popperfoto; Barna Tanko/iStock Editorial/Getty Images Plus; John W Banagan/Photographer's Choice; Pattilabelle/iStock/Getty Images Plus; SAM YEH/AFP; Jeffrey Greenberg/Universal Images Group; QQ7/iStock/Getty Images Plus; yogysic/DigitalVision Vectors; elenaleonova/E+; DonNichols/E+; mukesh-kumar/iStock/Getty Images Plus; Jupiterimages/Photolibrary; KatarzynaBialasiewicz/iStock/Getty Images Plus; Studio_Dagdagaz/iStock/Getty Images Plus; bonchan/iStock/Getty Images Plus; ChesiireCat/iStock/Getty Images Plus; Roberto Ricciuti/WireImage; rusm/E+; chameleonseye/iStock Editorial/Getty Images Plus; chameleonseye/iStock/Getty Images Plus; QQ7/iStock/Getty Images Plus; Hulton Archive; Popperfoto; Bloomberg; Bruno Vincent/Staff/Getty Images News.

Front cover by Hero Images; Eva-Katalin/E+. Back cover by Monty Rakusen/Cultura.
The following images are sourced from other libraries:
U1: Frank Veronsky; Media Bakery; MBI/Alamy; **U2:** FogStock/Alamy; Frank Veronsky; Kathy deWitt/Alamy; **U3:** Shutterstock; Photo Library; **U4:** AP/Wide World Photos; Frank Veronsky; George Kerrigan; Douglas Keister; Shutterstock; Reuters; Alamy; Scott Jenkins; **U5:** Frank Veronsky; **U6:** Frank Veronsky; CBS/Everett Collection; **U7:** Shutterstock; Frank Veronsky; Photo Edit; **U8:** Shutterstock; Media Bakery; Scott Olson; **U9:** NASA; AP/Wide World Photos; Frank Veronsky; AP/Wide World Photos; Newscom; Media Bakery; AP/Wide World Photos; **U10:** Shutterstock; Martin Lee/Alamy; Media Bakery; Carlos Davila/Alamy; Frank Veronsky; Ninja Akasaka; Jack Carey/Alamy; **U11:** Media Bakery; Inmagine; **U12:** Media Bakery; Shutterstock; Frank Veronsky; Courtesy of Suzanne Lefebre; **End Matter:** Shannon99/Alamy; US mint; Media Bakery; Adventure House; Shutterstock; Everett Collection; Mary Evans Picture Library/Everett Collection; Newscom.

Illustration
Front Matter: John Goodwin; Kim Johnson; **U1:** QBS Learning; John Goodwin; **U2:** QBS Learning; Kim Johnson; **U3–7:** QBS Learning; **U9:** Rob Schuster; **U11–12, End Matter:** QBS Learning.

QBS Learning pp5, 16, 19, 20, 21, 23, 30, 31, 32, 36, 40, 46, 49, 50, 59, 60, 66, 69, 70, 71, 106, 110, 111, 119, 128, 130, 133, 134, 135, 140, 144

Art direction, book design, and layout services: QBS Learning
Audio production: CityVox, NYC and John Marshall Media
Video production: Steadman Productions